THE POLICE AND THE GHETTO

Kennikat Press
National University Publications
Multi-disciplinary Studies in the Law

Advisory Editor
Honorable Rudolph J. Gerber

JOHN L. COOPER

THE

POLICE

AND THE

GHETTO

National University Publications
KENNIKAT PRESS // 1980
Port Washington, N.Y. // London

Manufactured in the United States of America

Published by
Kennikat Press Corp.
Port Washington, N.Y. / London

Library of Congress Cataloging in Publication Data

Cooper, John L   1936-
    The police and the ghetto.

    (Multidisciplinary studies in law) (National university publications)
    Bibliography: p.
    1. Police—United States. 2. Public relations—
Police. 3. Afro-American police. 4. United States—
Race relations. I. Title.
HV8138.C65   363.2   79-19261
ISBN 0-8046-9250-5

For Estelle, Melanie, and Armin

CONTENTS

THE POLICE AND THE GHETTO

John L. Cooper is Associate Professor of Sociology and Black Studies and Chairman of the Black Studies Department at John Jay College of Criminal Justice in New York City. A native of Philadelphia, he has long been interested in urban police problems.

CHAPTER 1

INTRODUCTION

The role of the police in the ghetto is beset with ambiguities, not the least of which is: What should be their primary function? We live in a society where crime is omnipresent and appears to be institutionalized. The ghetto is seen as a major source of crime. Therefore, should the role of the police in the ghetto be that of guardian-warriors; that is, should they be instruments of prevention against lawlessness and disorder? Should they be expected to prevent crime in the ghetto or just contain it there? Or, should their role be basically a protective function, that of protecting the *haves* from the *have nots*—which essentially means protecting the white middle class from a permanently impoverished black and brown underclass. And most importantly, should the police in the ghetto be guided by society's humanitarian values, or must their behavior be piloted by a self-righteous "I am better than they" pragmatism?

Such questions are not easily answered, if for no other reason than the fact that historically the role of the police has been an ever changing one in our society. However, a cursory acquaintance with police activities in the ghetto today would suggest that the role played there is likely to include all these attitudes and attributes. Clearly, it is a complex role. Therefore, it is the purpose of this study to investigate the complex nature of the police role in the ghetto.

But before going directly to our subject, a few general remarks need to be made. It is the purpose of these remarks to point out that the role of the police in the ghetto does not begin in the ghetto. It only ends there. If we want to understand this end, then we have to try to start at the beginning.

First, there is a much larger issue behind the question of what should be

3

the role of the police in the ghetto. The larger issue is: What should be the role of the police in a democratic society? This question became a matter of great concern a decade ago because of the extraordinary social activism that erupted in the ghetto during the 1960s. The civil rights marches and the ghetto riots, which brought on accommodating and confrontation responses from the law enforcement establishment, demonstrated that police power can be a force for liberation or repression. This suggests that police power can swing all too easily from one end of the political spectrum to the other, and we can conclude from this that police power, by its very nature, is a manipulative tool of society.

In this context, and in a broad general sense, police power is but an extension of our society's will and our society's values. From this vantage point, questions about the role of the police in our society would be better served if framed around Jerome H. Skolnick's focus of inquiry in his book *Justice Without Trial* in which he asks: "What values do the police serve in a democratic society?" Consequently, any question on the role of the police in the ghetto must inevitably give strong consideration to those values the police do seem to serve.

Second, the role of the police is constantly influenced by the public being served, which also includes the social environment that contains that public. For the cop on the streets in particular, this means that his behavior is being greatly influenced by the people on his beat and the streets he must patrol. But also, his public includes his buddies and fellow officers who share his successes, failures, and frustrations; and as well, more than ever today, his public takes into account his spokesmen—the politicians, the academicians, and the news reporters.

At the same time, it is to be understood that the policeman comes to his job with certain influences already built into his personality. These influences are matters of belief, class attitudes, and sociocultural values that the policeman may have had since he was a child. Therefore, the role of the cop on the beat tends to reflect a dialectic between two distinct modes of socialization, the primary socialization that the cop encountered when he was growing up, and a secondary socialization that comes from acting out the role of a cop.

Finally, it is the purpose of this book to discuss the role of the police in the ghetto. The term ghetto is being used here in a generic sense. Because of America's pluralism there are those who would say that our country is a nation of many different types of ghettos. That proposition is arguable, but nevertheless the black ghetto is our reference point for this study. While it is recognized that there are certainly differences in the black ghettos of America, say, between Watts in Los Angeles and Harlem in New York, they are still the same in their most important respect. They all house a rejected nonwhite, black population that has been declared unfit to live with their white betters, and unfit to participate equally and fully in the society as a whole. The role of the police in the ghetto is also a fact of this reality.

BACKGROUND

In recent years there has been a great deal of widespread public and academic interest in law enforcement in America. This interest was sparked by the tumultuous social upheavals of the sixties, which also just happened to be accompanied by a rapidly rising crime rate throughout the nation. There was the Civil Rights Movement, the ghetto riots in Newark, Detroit, and Los Angeles, as well as in other cities, and there was the Student Activist Movement and the Anti-Vietnam War Protest.

Black and white joined hands to fight the establishment. They took to the streets to challenge the wisdom of government policy and the legitimacy of government action. Discussion and debate gave way to tear gas, clubs, and guns as the means for resolving social and political differences. The streets of America's urban centers and the campuses of some of this nation's finest universities became battlegrounds that were displayed on television to the nation and the world. Overnight the potential "criminal" population took a quantum leap, and it embraced large segments of the American society, in particular those who were not white or who were of college age.

The very structure of the American society was shaken. The nation seemed to be teetering on the brink of social chaos and anarchy. Richard Nixon was elected president in 1968 in part because of his strong stand for "law and order," and it was this same public attitude that pushed the police to the forefront. They were now seen as the nation's first line of defense against this internal threat to security. This "visibility led to popular interest, television shows, movies, and social controversy. The city was to become America's new frontier, and the police were romanticized into asphalt cowboys, riding the range of urban crime and disorder." Moreover, it was clearly the urban ghetto which was being seen largely as this new frontier.

As the nation was being rocked by antiestablishment protest and demonstrations, the crime rate was jumping upward dramatically. FBI statistics for 1964 indicated that the overall rate for major crimes such as murder, rape, robbery, aggravated assault, burglary, and automobile theft were up 13 percent. The rate increased another 6 percent in 1965, 11 percent in 1966, and 17 percent in 1967. The fact of the matter was that major crimes were increasing faster than the population. These statistics further aggravated the sense of insecurity that lay over the nation.

As might have been suspected, the crime rates in the large cities were much higher than in other areas of the country, and within those large cities the highest crime rates were being recorded in the disadvantaged black neighborhoods. "In 1966, 1,754 [major] crimes were reported to police for every 100,000 Americans. In cities over 250,000, the rate was 3,153, and in cities over one million, it was 3,630—or more than double the national average. In suburban areas alone, including suburban cities, the rate was only 1,300, or just over one-third the rate in the largest cities."[1]

The weight of these numbers had begun to spell out a frightening truth. Crime had become a basic dynamic of urban living. At the same time, crime in the black disadvantaged areas of the large cities was being accepted as an institutionalized characteristic of the community. As a consequence, it would seem that the asphalt cowboys would have to ride herd on the ghetto if America was to combat insurrection and crime in the streets. And, for all practical purposes, the turf of the number one "domestic enemy," crime and disorder, had been defined. Moreover, in this case the turf also defined the enemy's cohorts and willing conspirators.

In effect, the term "rising crime rates" became a euphemism for the ghetto, and to that degree the urban ghetto became a kind of symbol for all the social travails of the sixties. Indeed, one might suspect that the more conservative elements in the country at that time, the law and order faction, the "silent majority" faction that backed Richard Nixon for president, and the far right-winger types like members of the John Birch Society, actually thought of the ghetto as a creeping cancer that was infecting the whole of American society with the disease of crime.

It was easy enough to be of such a mind in the mid-1960s. Americans had long been aware of the higher rates of crime in the ghetto, but now those higher rates were beginning to spread more generally throughout the society. Further, it was widely believed that much of the increase in predatory crime was the result of heroin addicts out to get money to support their habits. And where did the heroin addicts come from? Well, heroin addiction was still being seen as primarily a problem of the ghetto.

But even more telling for the conservative forces was the spreading use of heroin beyond the ghetto. During the sixties, heroin addiction was beginning to show up in higher frequency among middle-class white youths. Many such white youths had participated in civil rights marches and had taken part in social programs in the ghetto. Were these middle-class white youths learning the drug habit from lower-class black youths? Undoubtedly, some Americans believed that this was the case. In this regard, James Q. Wilson had the following to say:

Social programs designed to combat poverty brought together groups that once would have been isolated from each other, and thus spread the contagion as surely as bringing men together in the Army during World War 1 spread the influenza epidemic. The contacts of upper-middle-class suburban youths with ghetto blacks as a result of civil rights programs increased access to the drug culture, or perhaps created in the eyes of whites the mistaken view that such a "culture" existed, and was desirable, when in fact only deviant and episodic drug taking existed.[2]

The ghetto was something upon which society could vent its reactions. It was much more specific than the amorphous protest and street demonstrations that tended to come and go with the arousal and subsiding of the ire of antiestablishment forces. The ghetto was permanent, with specific dimensions that could be evaluated and measured for data collection purposes, data like drug and crime statistics, and this information could be used to formulate definite policies that might lead to remedial and corrective actions.

It is to be understood that the unrest of the sixties was bringing about a new social focus on the ghetto. It was not an entirely new process, but it was one with new social emphasis. The ghetto had fallen hostage, once again, to the social deviant labeling process. It had been defined as the camp of the enemy, a community of institutionalized deviancy, and as a result proclaimed as a community of outsiders. Therefore, it was to be seen as isolated from the "normal" community. In labeling the ghetto as the turf of the enemy, policymakers and the agents for social control were shifting societal emphasis away from the civil rights marchers, the war protesters, the addicts, the criminals in the streets, to the institutions of law enforcement. A message was being given to the public: the sheriff is on the way to reestablish social order.

A psychology of action against the enemy had been established in the public's mind by the mid-1960s. A campaign was expected and the government obliged. In fact, the government had been preparing to take action against youth crime among urban Negroes since 1961 when President Kennedy's Committee on Juvenile Delinquency and Youth Crime had been established. The committee was to undertake projects to demonstrate and evaluate the most effective countermeasures to combat the galloping youth crime in the ghetto. The Committee on Juvenile Delinquency was actually the forerunner of the War on Poverty Program. The Office of Economic Opportunity's (OEO) community action approach was a direct descendant of the earlier program. To this extent, the War on Poverty was as much a program to combat crime as it was a program to help the disadvantaged uplift themselves from poverty.

The War on Poverty Program was enacted into law in 1964. In 1965, President Johnson in a message to Congress declared war on crime. The president said the trend towards lawlessness had to be reversed. Crime had become a malignant enemy in America. This presidential message was followed by the appointment of a special commission, the President's Commission on Law Enforcement and Administration of Justice in 1965, which issued its general report in February 1967: *The Challenge of Crime in a Free Society*. In July of 1967, President Johnson appointed another special commission, the National Advisory Commission on Civil Disorders. This commission specifically was to study the urban riots, or disorders, that had been occurring around the country since 1963. The president directed the Commission on Civil Disorders to produce "a profile of the riots—of the rioters, of their environment, of their victims, of their causes and effects."

The executive branch of government was doing its part in the campaign against crime and disorder, and in 1968 Congress complemented these efforts by enacting the Omnibus Crime Control and Safe Streets Act. In enacting this law, Congress said that the high rate of crime in the country threatened the peace, security, and general welfare of the nation and its people. Congress went on to say that crime was to be prevented through better coordination and intensification of law enforcement efforts at all levels of government.

Richard Quinney says that these government actions were producing a new form of crime control. "Not only was the war on crime intensified by legislation, presidential commissions, and policy research by liberal academicians, but the capitalist state was now instituting a new system of domestic control. Especially with the newly created federal agency, the Law Enforcement Assistance Administration (LEAA), with appropriations amounting to millions of dollars, all levels of government were involved in planning and implementing an apparatus to secure the existing capitalist order."[3]

One may argue with Quinney's politics, but he is correct in identifying this new focus of the government's anti-crime campaign. He also points out that new terminology was created. The campaign gave birth to the term criminal justice. It was in effect an updating of the law and order ideology, and a recognition of the new emphasis being placed on maintaining order through the tools and agencies of the establishment or, more specifically, the invested authorities of the institutions for social control: the nation's police network. "With the euphemism of criminal justice, within a decade a new system of control has been established and (at the same time) justified. Today we are all attuned in one way or another to criminal justice."

As the government intensified its war on crime, the voices from the ghetto that had been calling for social change grew more militant and the people structurally more military. It was not that the voices from the ghetto were specifically reacting to the label of enemy, but rather that the rising tones of the militants had more to do with the growing impatience of blacks with the system. The civil rights demonstrations and the War on Poverty Program were not bringing about the substantive changes that many blacks thought necessary if blacks were to better their conditions. As a result, a revolutionary fervor among a small faction of blacks took hold in the ghetto, and these militants called for a restructuring of the society which would lead to a redistribution of power and wealth. The talk of revolution in the ghetto further isolated the blacks from the normal white community, and made it more of an object for the new program of domestic control.

In the summer of 1966, Stokely Carmichael used the term "black power" and it immediately caught the public's imagination. To most people it meant a black takeover of society. Consistent with the black power theme, black activists began to advocate community control of schools and other local institutions like those of the health system. The blacks were saying, "If we cannot move out of the ghetto or integrate the schools, then let us at least control the institutions and services of the ghetto, including the schools." Many people in the government saw this call for community control as a direct result of the community action programs of the War on Poverty. Daniel P. Moynihan apparently believed this, for he said that government officials of the War on Poverty Program gave support to an ideology of "Power to the people!" This in turn gave support to the community control advocates. The blacks' call for community control and black power scared many whites into thinking that OEO was funding the criminal and disruptive social elements in the society. It was one of the factors that helped to turn public opinion against the War on Poverty Program.

The call for black power had yet another frightening effect upon whites; in particular, white politicians. Between 1940 and 1966, there had been a tremendous black population shift from Southern rural areas to metropolitan urban areas. "In 1966, 69 percent of all Negroes were not only living in metropolitan areas rather than rural areas, but 37 percent (compared to 22 percent in 1940, 34 percent in 1960) were living in the North, most of them in cities."[4] The central cities of metropolitan areas were becoming, so it seemed in the mid-1960s, black and ghettoized. In numbers alone, the blacks were already overwhelming the cities. Black political power, which could lead to black community control of local institutions, seemed to be on the verge of becoming a reality in the large urban centers.

In 1966, blacks comprised 26 percent of the population in cities of one million or more, as compared to 13 percent in 1950. Only 4 percent of the suburban population was black. Blacks were increasing as a percentage of the total population in almost all of the big cities. In New York City, blacks comprised 10 percent of the population in 1950, 18 percent estimated in 1965; in Los Angeles, 9 percent in 1950, 17 percent in 1965; and in Chicago, they comprised 14 percent in 1950, and 28 percent in 1965.

Using 1965 estimates, the fifteen cities with the largest percentages of blacks were, in the following order:

Washington, D.C.	66%	Detroit	34%
Newark	47%	Cleveland	34%
Atlanta	44%	Philadelphia	31%
New Orleans	41%	Chicago	28%
Memphis	40%	Cincinnati	24%
Baltimore	38%	Indianapolis	23%
St. Louis	36%	Houston	23%
	Kansas City 22%		

The National Advisory Commission on Civil Disorders (Kerner Commission) stated that whereas the black population in 1966 in all central cities totaled more than 12 million, the black population in these cities would rise by 1985 to more than 20 million. This would mean that 66 percent of all blacks would be central city residents. These were awesome and frightening figures to a society that had judged the enemy turf to be the inner city ghettos, and the fact that many of the cities with large black populations did experience riots seemed to more than confirm the designation that the ghettos were enemy camps.

However, when the Black Panthers appeared in the ghetto, all the worst fears of white America—the enemy was indeed in its midst—seemed about to become a reality. Here was a black paramilitary group, Marxist in orientation, which called for blacks to unite for a violent struggle with the oppressive white society. Their slogan was "political power comes from the barrel of a gun," a saying that was taken from the political philosophy of Mao Tse Tung. Also, the fact that the minister of information of the Panthers, Eldridge Cleaver, was a convicted rapist seemed to tie the criminal element for many whites to the blacks' call for social change. And, after the Panthers had had bloody shoot-outs with the police, the proof of the pudding was clearly discernable to all who were willing to acknowledge it. Names like Huey Newton, Bobby Seale, and Eldridge Cleaver became household words.

It was in 1966 that the Black Panther Party for Self-Defense was organized. The group's purpose was to follow the police around in the ghetto on the lookout for police mistreatment of blacks. It was different from a similar group in Los Angeles known as the Community Alert Patrol in that the Panthers carried and openly displayed weapons, a practice that was not illegal at the time.

The Panthers had come suddenly to the public's attention on February 1, 1967, when twenty of them, armed with pistols and shot-guns, marched through San Francisco International Airport to escort Malcolm X's wife to a speaking engagement. The reason they gave for the armed escort was a belief they held that the same forces which had assassinated her husband might make an attempt on her life. "It was not until May 1967, however, when the California legislature debated a bill calling for a prohibition against the carrying of weapons, that the Panthers achieved national prominence by appearing within the state capitol armed to the teeth."[5]

Looking back on that Panther incident of May 1967, one can recall the shock waves that gust through the nation. "My God," was the sentiment. The enemy was marching out of the ghetto and taking the initiative. "Who in the hell were these crazies? Where did they really come from?"

Whites genuinely did not understand the Panthers. They knew so little about ghetto social types that they could not clearly "see" them. Very few whites had experienced the ghetto or had interacted with its residents. Whites who did frequent the ghetto played roles that did not encourage insight into the nature of the social system. Their roles were as agents of various kinds of bureaucracies—policemen, social workers, teachers. If whites gave any thought to the term "black ghetto," a variety of images suggesting danger and degradation probably sprang to mind. Whites did know that the Panthers were not civil rights blacks of the Martin Luther King-Roy Wilkins type with whom whites could identify, nor were Panthers long suffering victims of the freedom rider type with whom whites could sympathize. The Panthers were sharply, though exotically, dressed blacks who carried guns; and not knowing the right category, whites placed them in the only category they had. The Panthers were placed in the category of "crazy niggers."

The Panthers also called up another fear that has long manifested itself in white America. The ghetto, and in particular black people, are still very much a mystery to whites. And as is frequently the case we tend to fear something which has an influence on our lives and which we do not understand. The Panthers came to symbolize the slinking monster in the dark that most whites visualized as the nature of the ghetto.

The Panthers, vocally, and physically when necessary, took on the police, and in the drama these two groups played out, the police were perceived by most whites as heroes, as defenders of the community against a savage horde. Whereas, police chief Eugene "Bull" Connor had been seen as a sadistic Neanderthal when he turned water hoses and dogs on black civil rights marchers in the early 1960s, Edward V. Hanrahan was praised by whites a decade later after he directed a raid by Chicago police on an apartment where two Panthers were killed and four others wounded under circumstances that strongly suggest that the police met little or no resistance.

No doubt, ideologically speaking, the Panthers were radical, but other radical groups were not subjected to attack. To be sure, there is little evidence that Panther ideology was even remotely understood by the public. The Panthers were repeatedly called racist, although they repudiated black separatism and sought a coalition of the oppressed and of those who opposed capitalism. To them capitalism was the problem rather than whites.

To whites in America it did not matter what was the true ideology of the Panthers. They had become a symbol for the crime and disorder in the ghetto that was indeed affecting the whole of society. If America was to be saved, the insurgency had to be stopped. So, a nation turned its head while the asphalt cowboys used vigilante tactics, and by 1971 the Panthers were in disarray. The revolt in the ghetto had been arrested. Most of the national leadership of the party were dead, in jail, or in exile. The remnants of the party were regrouping to work within the system, at least for the present. An indication of this could be seen in the fact that Black Panther leader Bobby Seale ran for mayor of Oakland, California in 1973.

The persecution of the Black Panthers was direct and unmistakable. The head of the party, Huey Newton, was sent to jail on a trumped-up voluntary manslaughter charge. Eldridge Cleaver's house was raided by the police and a few months later his parole was revoked and he was ordered back to jail. Cleaver fled the country as a fugitive from justice. Bobby Seale was sentenced to forty-eight months in jail by Judge Julius Hoffman, three months on each of sixteen charges. Seale was sentenced this way in order to evade a Supreme Court decision that said any person imprisoned for more than six months was entitled to a jury trial. A number of Panthers were arrested in New York City and held in jail on very high bail for over a year, and in December of 1969, two Panthers, Fred Hampton and Mark Clark, were killed and four others wounded by the Chicago police in the previously mentioned incident.

As the 1960s drew to a close, the streets of the nation, and even more so the streets of the ghetto, had grown considerably more quiet and orderly. Protest demonstrations were still going on against the Vietnam War but with considerably less radicalism. Gone were the huge, emotional civil rights marches; the calls from the ghetto for social change had been largely stifled. However, the fears that had been generated by ghetto uprisings were still kept very much alive behind the euphemism of rising crime rates. This task, perhaps inadvertently, fell to the academic stalwarts who rushed to the banner of criminal justice. They could easily rationalize their efforts as a search for knowledge in a virgin field. *Theirs was to be value-free research.*

The role and influence of the academicians in keeping the public's eyes and ears attuned to the dangers of the ghetto in the latter sixties and now the seventies should not be minimized in the least. To begin with, academic types were plentifully represented as directors, consultants, and advisors to the presidential commissions in the 1960s that dealt with crime and disorder. For example, the influence of Lloyd E. Ohlin, the criminologist, on the conclusions of the President's Commission on Law Enforcement and Administration of Justice is very well known. It is this commission which helped to give birth to the Omnibus Crime Control and Safe Streets Act.

But more specifically, academicians have come to be accepted as having a direct, legitimate role to play in law enforcement, and it has thereby greatly increased their range of influence in the criminal justice system. This has been a recent development, and in its own way it is a kind of backlash of the crime and disorder of the sixties. James Q. Wilson points out one of the more important reasons for this recent development:

. . . in the mid-1960s, and perhaps today as well, social scientists concerned with crime shared a common perspective, but not one that emphasized the material condition of society; that this shared perspective led to a policy stalemate and an ethical dilemma; that when social scientists were asked for advice by national policymaking bodies, they could not respond with suggestions derived from and supported by their scholarly work; and that as a consequence such advice as was supplied tended to derive from their general political views as modified by their political and organizational interaction with those policy groups and their staffs.[6]

However, as Richard Quinney points out, in the mid-1960s a new form of emphasis was being placed on maintaining order through the tools and agencies of the nation's police network. The public and the law enforcement institutions needed to be educated quickly to this new emphasis because events in the mid-1960s were moving rapidly. As a consequence, the academicians became very necessary to this developing effort. And, the government was not ungenerous in rewarding academicians and their institutions for the role they were being called upon to play.

Says Quinney, the new technology required an educated and indoctrinated personnel and academic programs in criminal justice. Such programs have developed rapidly in the last decade. The federal government, using the Crime Control and Safe Streets Act of 1968, authorized LEAA to make grants and loans to criminal justice personnel and to those who planned to be employed in the criminal justice system. LEAA's major educational program, the Law Enforcement Education Program (LEEP), provided financial support for the college education of persons employed in law enforcement, courts, corrections, and other criminal justice agencies. More than 200,000 students have received financial support from LEEP since the program began. The program has grown immensely, from 20,602 students in 485 colleges and universities, to more than 95,000 students in 1,036 schools. The budget for these programs has increased from $6.5 million in 1969 to more than $84 million in 1976 for manpower development. LEAA provides funds for criminal justice graduate programs, sponsors a graduate research fellowship program, and provides funds to enable college students to work in criminal justice agencies, thus promoting an interest in future criminal justice careers.[7]

With the emphasis on education in the criminal justice system, teachers became spokesmen for the new ideology with their classroom instruction, their research, their papers, and books. To this extent, they were and are opinion makers, if not directly to the public then through their students and government policymakers who were supporting the educational mission of the new criminal justice ideology. If this new form of maintaining order was being directed, covertly as such, at the ghetto, then the academicians were in an excellent position to influence the policy. Moreover, as teachers, and to that degree trainers of law enforcement personnel, academicians were in a position to have much to say about the role of the police in the ghetto.

The criminal justice academicians came from a wide spectrum of disciplines, and were for the most part liberal in their personal attitudes and political outlooks. Nevertheless, their studies and research constituted in large measure an ongoing reaffirmation of the ghetto as a community of institutionalized deviancy. To be sure, on a much smaller scale, this process had begun considerably earlier in academia, particularly in the field of sociology, with such individuals as Robert K. Merton, "Social Structure and Anomie" (1938), Albert K. Cohen, *Delinquent Boys: The Culture of the Gang* (1955), Edwin H. Sutherland and Donald R. Cressey, *Principles of Criminology* (1960), Richard A. Cloward and Lloyd E. Ohlin, *Delinquency and Opportunity* (1960). While the works of these men may not have concentrated on the black ghetto per se, the ghetto was being labeled by implication because they all tended to talk about the reasons for deviance among the lower classes. Therefore, these earlier labeling practices were much more general in nature and emphasized a functionalist approach to the understanding of deviancy among the lower classes.

However, the new adherents to the criminal justice ideology in academia are much more forthright in directly associating much of their work with the ghetto and crime control by the police in that community. Their work seems to constitute a watch over the ghetto, to the point that an intellectual of this new academic wave, James Q. Wilson, feels it necessary to debunk earlier ideas and theories on crime that would seem to suggest that the ghetto, in and of itself, does not necessarily cause crime.

Under the new wave of academic interest in criminal justice, researchers are exploring all aspects of law enforcement and its relationship to society. They study police administration, police-community relations, the courts, the legal system, crime and its manifestations in modern society, recidivism, psychological profiles of the police, and many different facets of deviancy, just to mention a few of the topics. Nonetheless, one should not be misled by topic and title headings. A brief review of the literature points out that much of the present research is being done with the ghetto in mind. Studies in police-community relations clearly state this case, and this area of study just happens to dominate the literature. But most importantly, it is the characterization of the ghetto as a dangerous, volatile, hostile environment, particularly in respect to the police, that shows that the new-wave academicians are carrying on the process of labeling the ghetto as a deviant community, even if the labeling is unintended and inadvertent.

What makes this academic labeling process very important to law enforcement is the fact that today there is a large number of individuals in college who are employed in that system, many of whom are likely to be getting their education at the behest of LEAA or LEEP. If the teachers in the classrooms are labeling the ghetto, then students are likely to do the same because the opinions of teachers are much too readily accepted. And if nothing else, students may have to read these characterizations of the ghetto for their classroom work and outside research. If these students do not already have an opinion, it is not too much to assume that these characterizations may well leave certain negative impressions on their minds. Just a few of those academic descriptions will readily illustrate how the academicians are carrying on the process of labeling the ghetto.

To begin with, pointing out the high rate of crime among blacks as compared to whites always serves to demonstrate the dangerous character of the ghetto, but it also immediately implies the need for closer police control and supervision of ghetto residents, frequently in the name of the ghetto residents themselves. There is also a tacit suggestion in this latter point that blacks recognize their own inability to maintain order in their communities. The following is a "high rate of crime among blacks" presentation:

The incidence of crimes among Negroes is disproportionately high, especially with regard to crimes of violence. The president's crime commission report indicates that the arrest rate of Negroes for FBI Index Offenses in 1965 was four times as great as that for whites; the Negro arrest rate for murder was almost ten times as high; and for burglary it was almost three and one-half times as high. We may not conclude from this, however, that a tendency toward crime is a genetic quality inherent in Negroes. One variable accounting for the disparity between white and Negro crime rates is a difference in level of income. There is a strong correlation between poverty (and especially slum living) and crime, and Negroes are disproportionately poor. Studies of ethnic groups in America have shown that crime rates decrease as the group moves from the core city to the suburbs. The difference in arrest rates between Negroes and whites living under similar conditions is far less disparate.[8]

Another illustration indicates how academic researchers tend to have a penchant for underscoring what they see as the volatile nature of the ghetto. It serves as a reminder of the urban riots of the sixties, and the uncontrolled nature of blacks. The crime rates indicate that blacks are extraordinarily aggressive and willfully predatory. The public has to be on guard. The ghetto is filled with crazy niggers who are always ready to turn on those who would help them. The following is a statement of this type of description:

Like many other social problems, the level of tension between police and community seems to follow a gradient. At the outer suburbs the relation is cool, but as the observer moves towards the inner city, the gradient signals red hot. Where harmony between police and ghetto seemingly exists, it is a temporary facade that barely camouflages the endemic and permanent core of reciprocal antagonism. These pockets of resentment are mutually aggravating, and it makes no difference that many of them are exaggerated.[9]

Continually looking at the negative side of the ghetto can cause researchers to conclude and/or imply that in the final analysis blacks are very much responsible for their problems of crime, disorder, and police brutality. For example, a study that was done for the National Advisory Commission on Civil Disorders concluded that blacks, at all age levels, were much more likely than whites to be critical of the police. Blacks were more prone to believe that the police used insulting language towards them, frisked and searched them for no reason, and that police tended to rough them up. Are blacks, like children, supersensitive? Certainly, it is to be understood that crazy niggers are unable to keep cool heads, and just as there are white bigots, there are also black bigots. The following illustration is offered:

It is incontestable that for better relations with minority groups the police must constantly improve their record in civil rights. But such improvement, though necessary, may not be sufficient. Rapprochement must come from two sides and requires an ideological shift by the minority group. As long as Negroes comprise an alienated ghetto society, the police will symbolize to them all that is detestable in an oppressive white social system. It becomes a vicious circle as the police respond in kind and the beating of arrested Negroes often serves as a vengeance for the fears and perils the policemen are subjected to while pursuing their duties in the Negro community.[10]

Yet, another example points out that the academic literature can sometimes give the impression that blacks actually work against reducing crime in the cities. Since most crime in the cities, according to FBI statistics, occurs in the ghetto this is tantamount to saying that blacks accept, if not want, crime in their communities. Amitai Etzioni believes that deviant behavior in the ghetto is one of the means by which the residents adapt to their poverty. He says that "the poor adapt to poverty by resorting to illegal activity that their subculture legitimates, such as bookmaking, prostitution and drug peddling." It is a way for them to satisfy their material craving, says Etzioni. But is this not also saying that therefore the ghetto is a community of institutionalized deviancy, and that ghetto residents place a positive value on certain forms of crime? And if a positive value is placed on illegal activities, one can imagine that ghetto residents would protect their rights to resort to them. This ambience was presented in the motion picture *The Cross and the Switchblade*. All of this seems to say that crime is inevitable in the ghetto, and the people there are willing to fight to keep it that way.

The most important part of the following example is the content in between the lines: "Without community cooperation the job of reducing crime in the cities is virtually impossible. The policeman knows it. He knows that without friends there, the ghetto is an unsafe and hostile enemy camp. But when he tries to bridge the gap, he finds it difficult and often impossible to communicate."[11]

Of course, there are the hardliners who step forward to tell it like it is. They do not hide behind the metaphor or the in-between lines commentary. They not only blame the ghetto for most of its problems, but they like to chastise government, the do-gooders, the bleeding heart liberals who think that government intervention in ghetto life may serve to ameliorate some of the problems of poverty's vicious cycle. The hardliners tend to fall behind the position taken by William Graham Sumner almost a hundred years ago when he said that the liberal Northern do-gooders did more harm than good when they forced the South into freeing the slaves by way of the Civil War. If there was to be any change in the relationship between master and slave, then this had to be done by the people of the South, and it was not to be forced on them by the people of the North. In the same way, the hardliners believe that if there is to be any change in the ghetto, say in respect to crime, then it is the residents of the ghetto who must take responsibility for it. If the ghetto residents are not willing to do what is necessary to change their lives—for the better, it is assumed—then let them suffer. They are only getting what they deserve.

The following is a good statement of the hardliner's position:

During the 1960s, bad police-community relations were described as a chief cause of black riots. The police were variously described as an "army of occupation" and "pigs," the neighborhood residents as "rioters" and "lawless" or worse. At the height of the concern, it seemed as if the inner cities were in a perpetual state of war, and in some places that was not very far from the truth.

If matters were always and everywhere this bad, then nothing could be done. One cannot ameliorate with government programs a problem that arises out of the rejection of the legitimacy of government itself. If police and cities are, in the slums, implacable enemies utterly beyond reconciliation, then all the talk of improving matters with community relations programs, better trained officers, and more effective "communication" seems pointless and trivial.[12]

Then, there are the academic researchers who study the ghetto and come away generally frightened by the results of their own findings. The fear that has been generated within them may be so great thay they feel compelled to try to frighten the hell out of anyone who reads their material. They can be so swayed by their own fears that they become doomsayers, inadvertently shouting "the black peril is upon us!" They tend to see the crime situation in the ghetto as being out of hand, with no solution in sight. This can cause them to portray the situation in the ghetto as society's ultimate battleline. What happens in the ghetto is destined to determine the fate of American society. Both combatants, as they see it, are equally up against the wall. These presentations are essentially a cry for help. We, the people of the United States, they shout, are wandering around on a mined battleground, and there is no exit.

While these doomsayers see their research as focusing on a situational context, like that of the relationship between law enforcement and the ghetto, their attention overall tends to fall on the ghetto and its residents. The people of the ghetto will appear as intractable, implacable minions who are driven by forces totally beyond their control. The forces may be seen as ensuing from the overall nature of the society in economic and political terms, or from the overall nature of the ghetto community in terms of Oscar Lewis's "culture of poverty" and the psychic damage done to blacks by centuries of racism and discrimination. Either way, it doesn't matter much. For whites in American society, the alternatives are few. Hold the line! Hide behind the club and gun of the police and de facto segregation or wall up the minions in the ghetto like the Nazis did to the Jews in Poland.

Even the dialectic tone in the following statement does not quiet the doomsayer's message:

Many policemen feel their lives are in danger when they enter the black community, and many segments of the black community regard police-men as a repressive force. The hostility has become open and emotions are high. The accumulation of fire power by both groups can be used to support the charge and countercharge of armed insurrection and genocide. The self-defensive measures taken by police are understandable, as is the sense of repression felt by an increasingly wider segment of the black community. In turn, both reactions contribute to the felt danger and result in defensive reactions, thereby creating a vicious circle which generates a momentum of its own.[13]

The characterizations of the ghetto just given suggest certain under-lying beliefs had a hand in shaping the academic research. We will return to these beliefs very shortly. But first, one could argue that the char-acterizations of the ghetto that have been presented are essentially accurate, as the researchers who made these statements apparently believed. However, these types of characterizations are not explanations and they add very little to our sum of knowledge about the ghetto. But the worst problem with the statements mentioned lies in the fact that they tend to follow a line of presumption more than fact. Why would researchers take this line? Well, the statements can obviously be used to excite and draw attention to a researcher's work, and they can frequently prepare the reader for a certain type of descriptive reporting, one that may lean very heavily upon emotionalism rather than intellectual analysis. In fact, what usually follows in such works is not an analysis, but rather a comparative juxtaposition between the white and black communities.

In this context, for example, and only comparatively speaking, crime rates are higher in the ghetto. Of necessity, or so it would seem, this comparative fact gives rise to many negative characterizations of the ghetto, and such characterizations invariably make all white communities look better, as they relate to crime, than they really are. One would suppose that when whites read about "the rampant crime in the ghetto" they feel more secure and socially better off than blacks, and it is not too much to suspect that for some whites their feelings of being superior to blacks are confirmed. Is it that the labeling of black people can take on a genetic quality?

Now let us return to the underlying beliefs that seem to have taken a hand in shaping the academic literature discussed earlier. In respect to blacks and the ghetto, there is much to suggest that the criminal justice, community relations literature plays upon the social Darwinist attitudes that still exist in the mythology of American culture. Indeed, it should be said that social Darwinist undercurrents are displayed across much of the criminal justice literature in quiet, covert form, which is to say, its usual form. The attitudes that are being alluded to here are those which were so passionately expressed by William Graham Sumner in his defense of slavery in the South prior to the Civil War,[14] and it was these same attitudes that were given cinematic treatment by D. W. Griffith in his motion picture *Birth of a Nation*. Social Darwinism encompasses the beliefs that form the basis for America's black stereotype.

Sumner argued that in the South, prior to the Civil War, blacks and whites had formed habits of actions and feelings towards one another that produced a tranquil, contented lifestyle, if not a happy one. Both groups grew up in ways that were traditional and customary. There was an acceptance of the social roles each had to play in recognition of their inner dependency on the Southern slave system. In effect, they needed each other in the particular roles they had to play in order to survive. Survival being paramount, peace therefore prevailed. But this peaceful existence was disrupted by the Civil War in which the Northerners attempted to force a new lifestyle and new forms of relationships between the blacks and whites. The war failed to bring about this change, and as a consequence the war made enemies of the two peoples who had formerly lived in harmony.

Certainly, the implication of Sumner's argument has to be that whites and blacks were both better off, in terms of relating to one another for the good of Southern society, if not for the good of the entire American society, when blacks were in servitude, dominated and controlled by whites. Sumner doesn't say it, but his is the old white man's burden argument that blacks need the supervision and guidance of "the master." This is so, it is believed, because blacks are incapable of being responsible for themselves, which is also translated into the belief that blacks are basically shiftless, lazy, and childlike. Their childlike, irresponsible nature is taken as an indication that they have not come as far as whites along the human evolutionary track. Therefore, it is incumbent upon whites to govern the social apparatus and the social interaction between blacks and whites if they both should have their best chance of survival. These are the covert beliefs of social Darwinism.

It is not too difficult to imagine that some whites may well have seen a parallel between the turmoil of the sixties and the reconstruction period in the South in the last half of the nineteenth century. Romantically, whites can make a comparison between the tranquil years of the 1950s and the so-called tranquil years of the antebellum South. But, of course, in both cases the pictured tranquility was more fiction than fact. Then came the explosions of the sixties, like the Civil War, that tore apart the tranquil relationship between the races. After the Civil War, according to Griffith's film, the Klansmen had to rise to save the nation, but in the 1960s, we decided to rely upon the asphalt cowboys.

From Sumner's perspective, different social groups, like the Southerners and Northerners in the last century, inevitably develop different folkways and mores or different modes of social behavior. To be sure, this was seen as a major impetus in bringing on the Civil War. Because social Darwinism stresses the differences between blacks and whites, the presence of such attitudes in academic characterizations of the ghetto will, more than likely, stress the modes of behavior of blacks which differ from white behavior, rather than point out the modes of behavior of blacks which are similar to the behavior of whites. Thus, the academic characterizations can be judged as labeling the ghetto.

It is very easy for whites to give negative labels to the ghetto because they tend to have basic negative attitudes about blacks. They tend to hold to John Dollard's overall evaluation of the black community, an evaluation Dollard reached by surveying a black community in the South in the 1930s. Dollard concluded that black communities tend to precipitate aggression, and are socially freewheeling. Stanford Lyman concludes that Dollard really is saying that blacks are able "to practice life much nearer to its primordial psychobiological baseline: Blacks come closer to realizing the advantages of sexual freedom, emotional liberty, and unrestrained impulsiveness than do other higher-status groups." [13] Practicing life closer to its primordial baseline may be seen as socially advantageous according to Freud's notion that by its very nature society restricts basic human impulses, but to white Americans today this just points to the immorality and freewheeling deviancy in the black community. Essentially, what Dollard and Lyman are saying is that blacks in American society are being seen as borderline primitives.

If these social Darwinist attitudes are pervasive in American culture, then they are certainly operative in law enforcement, particularly, it would seem, for the cop whose beat is the ghetto. After all, "the socially defined role of the policeman toward the black community is a role dictated by the white community," and it is the white community which views blacks as borderline primitives. Moreover, it is true enough that the overwhelming majority of police officers who work in the ghetto are white.

Long discussions really are not needed on this point. But, of course, policemen are affected by this society's social Darwinist attitude. Jerome H. Skolnick gives this report made in 1951 from a Ph.D. thesis by William Westley. "For the police the Negro epitomizes the slum dweller and, in addition, he is culturally and biologically inherently criminal. Individual policemen sometimes deviate sharply from this general definition, but no white policeman with whom the author has had contact failed to mock the Negro, to use some type of stereotyped categorization, and to refer to interaction with the Negro in an exaggerated dialect when the occasion arose."[16]

Skolnick went on to say that Westley's characterization was true for all the police he studied on both the east and west coasts. He points out that during his tenure with a west coast police department he learned all the usual derisive terms referring to blacks and a great many other terms he had never heard before. The terms were used so frequently, the chief of police issued a directive stating as a matter of policy: "The following words and other similar derogatory words shall not be used by members and employees in the course of their official duties or at any other time." Included in the chief's statement was a litany of racial prejudice—"boy, spade, jig, nigger, blue, smoke, coon, spook, burr head, cat, black boy, black, shine, ape, spick, mau mau."

Further, studies have shown that policemen generally believe that blacks and some other ethnic minorities do require stricter enforcement procedures and rougher treatment than white members of the population. It is not surprising then that in a reported study of civilian complaints of police brutality in New York City in 1969, a large percentage of the authenticated instances of police brutality were brought by blacks and Puerto Ricans.[17]

Social Darwinism is an old story in America. Policemen, like the rest of us, have grown up with it. It is practically a basic element in our cultural ABC's. But more recently, the police role in the ghetto has been specifically influenced by the ghetto activism of the sixties. American society is still reacting to those events, and the police role in the ghetto today has to be seen, in goodly measure, as part of that reaction.

THE GHETTO

So far in this study we have been taking a look at some of the forces that are likely to influence police behavior in the ghetto. But as yet, we have not essentially discussed the most important of these forces, which is the ghetto itself. Up to now, we have been looking at the ghetto from a point outside of it, but this is obviously a limited, one-sided view. If we want to really understand the influence of the ghetto on the police role in that black community, then we need more of an understanding of what the ghetto is, and that calls for a larger perspective, one that includes a view from inside the ghetto itself.

First of all, the view of the ghetto as being a social accident must be dispelled. The ghetto did not appear in American cities in the willy-nilly fashion that politicians would have us believe. Ghettos have been a part of western European societies for many, many centuries as Louis Wirth pointed out in his book *The Ghetto*. The ghettos of Europe were used to segregate the Jews. The ghetto was a place for the unwanted and the rejected; those who were declared threats to the society, and therefore ghetto residents were both feared and despised.

Segregating people in ghettos, with all the restrictions and discrimination that go with it, has evolved as a legitimated sociocultural tool in modern society. It is an accepted way for a society to deal with a minority group population, although the society that does use it is not likely to acknowledge its purposes for doing so. The practice of enclosing people in ghettos is a part of America's cultural heritage, and it came to America in the hearts and minds of European immigrants. Now it is an institutionalized practice in urban America.

From another angle, there are those individuals who see the black ghetto as a colony. Kenneth B. Clark takes this position: "The dark ghettos are social, political, educational, and—above all—economic colonies. Their inhabitants are subject peoples, victims of the greed, cruelty, insensitivity, guilt, and fear of their masters." [18] Seeing the ghetto as a colony is to see it as no social accident. The European nations' quest for colonies in the last century was important to those nations' industrial development, and their quests were very much influenced by the social Darwinist beliefs in the inevitability of human evolutionary processes. Social struggle—between the races, not the classes—was the reality of the human world. It was nature's way of producing superior men. "Survival of the fittest!" Nineteenth-century imperialism proved that white people were superior to the black races, but that fact, imperialistically, must be proved over and over again. It is the struggle itself, and the winning, that keeps white people superior. So the ghetto, by sword, gun, club, or words, must be captured and subdued time and time again.

The following passage describes the genesis of this process in the ghetto as it occurred in the nineteenth century. Imperialism was strongly influenced and justified by evolutionary teachings. Competition and struggle were accepted as being a natural process in which survival was the ultimate goal. As the Europeans were successful at subjugating colonial peoples, this was proof in itself that the colonizers were by nature superior and more fit and therefore destined by the inevitable course of events to control the lands of the colored races. Their success justified any kind of action; the means by which it was achieved remained unimportant. To apply humanitarian policies to colonial peoples only upset or delayed the natural course of events, and the slogan "Blessed are the strong, for they shall prey upon the weak" characterized the whole movement.[19]

Let us take another view that rebukes the notion of the accidental presence of the ghetto in modern America. Robert Parks tells us that "every American city has its slums; its ghettos; its immigrant colonies, regions which maintain more or less alien and exotic culture. Nearly every large city has its bohemias and hobohemias, where life is freer, more adventurous and lonely than it is elsewhere. These are the so-called natural areas of the city." According to Parks, these natural areas were the basic building blocks of the cities.

They are the products of forces that are constantly at work to effect an orderly distribution of populations and functions within the urban complex. They are "natural" because they are not planned, and because the order that they display is not the result of design, but rather a manifestation of tendencies inherent in the urban situation; tendencies that city plans seek—though not always successfully—to control and correct. In short, the structure of the city, as we find it, is clearly just as much the product of the struggle and efforts of its people to live and work together collectively as are its local customs, traditions, social ritual, laws, public opinion, and the prevailing moral order.[20]

Parks seems to be saying that the natural order of the cities requires that there be ghettos. You could no more have American cities without ghettos than you could have fish living without water. Therefore, the people who live in the ghettos are not there because of rejection and discrimination, but rather they are there as a matter of the natural order of urban life. No ghettos, no cities, and, I might add, that since the modern way of life is built around cities, no ghettos, no modern way of life.

Why would the natural order of the cities require that blacks and other racial minorities live in ghettos? Parks said that what lends special importance to the segregation of the poor, the vicious, the criminal, and exceptional persons generally, which was so characteristic a feature of city life, is the fact that social contagion tends to stimulate in divergent types the same temperamental differences, and to suppress characters which unite them with the normal types about them. Being with people of their own ilk also provides not merely a stimulus, but a moral support for the traits they have in common which they would not find in a less select society. In the large urban areas the poor, the vicious, and the delinquent, crushed together in an unhealthy and contagious intimacy, breed in and in, soul and body, which led Parks to believe that those long genealogies of the Jukes and the tribes of Ishmael would not show such a persistent and distressing uniformity of vice, crime, and poverty unless they were peculiarly fit for the environment in which they were condemned to exist.[21]

Parks is saying that the only way American cities can exist is with the black people locked up in ghettos, kept there so their contagion will not spread to the normal types or, more specifically, to the white people around them.

There is a tremendous amount of economic poverty, ill health, dilapidated slum buildings, roaches, rats, and all other manners of social degradation in the ghetto. But they are all symptoms of the blacks' problems in America and not the problems themselves. The three views that address themselves to why there are ghettos in America, which are actually interrelated, suggest that the roots of the black problems in America are not in the ghetto at all. The roots are more likely to be found in the history, heritage, and culture of European peoples. The view of the ghetto from the ghetto, tends to reflect, along with bread and butter issues, this placement of the roots.

The aspect of ghetto life that tends to cut the deepest into black people is the sense of rejection by the rest of society. This sense of rejection attacks their psyches and ravages their spirits. The reason for this, in the first instance, comes from the fact that black people are not rejected because they are black, poor, aggressive, immoral, criminally oriented, or dirty. They are rejected because they are *nonwhite*. This is something that blacks cannot really understand because there is nothing in them that will allow them to understand in white terms what the human detriment is in being *nonwhite*. The exasperation and desperation for blacks in trying to understand the nonunderstandable leads them into feeling alienated, and as a consequence they are forced to experience anomie.

This sense of rejection has been written about in fiction and nonfiction form by many black writers: James Baldwin, *Nobody Knows My Name;* Chester Himes, *The Primitive;* Malcolm X, *The Autobiography of Malcolm X;* Eldrige Cleaver, *Soul on Ice,* just to mention a few. But one of the best descriptions of the all-consuming nature of this sense of rejection was written by the novelist Ralph Ellison.

Ellison wrote about a character in his novel *The Invisible Man* who could not relate to himself because he could not see himself. This brought about a moral dilemma for him. He said, "When one is invisible he finds such problems as good and evil, honesty, dishonesty, of such shifting shapes that he confuses one with the other, depending upon who happens to be looking through him at the time." Moreoever, the moral dilemma deepens when the invisible man attempts to look through himself. People around him do not like it when he attempts to expose this fact. They are more comfortable with lies, even though all find the lies dissatisfying. But when the invisible man attempts to "justify" and affirm someone's mistaken beliefs then he was loved and appreciated.

The invisible man goes on to say:

In my presence they could talk and agree with themselves, the world was nailed down, and they loved it. They received a feeling of security. But here was the rub: Too often, in order to justify them, I had to take myself by the throat and choke myself until my eyes bulged and my tongue hung out and wagged like the door of an empty house in a high wind. Oh yes, it made them happy and it made me sick. So I became ill of affirmation, of saying "yes" against the nay-saying of my stomach—not to mention my brain.

There is one essential fact about all colonized people. They are without power; power in social, economic, and political terms that can be used to determine their own destinies. Without that power, colonized people are but puppets and yo-yos on a string, to be played with and manipulated at the behest of the colonizers. The economics of the relationship is always second to the show of dominating strength over capitulating weakness. The call from the ghetto for black power in the 1960s was a challenge to this nexus as Martin Luther King, Jr. pointed out.

King said that black power, in its broad and positive meaning was a call to black people to amass the political and economic strengths necessary to achieve their legitimate goals. He said that no one could deny that blacks are in dire need of this kind of legitimate power. Indeed, one of the great problems that blacks confront is this lack of power. Going back to the old plantation days of the South to the present ghettos of the North, the blacks have been confined to a life of voicelessness and powerlessness. They have no power to make decisions about their lives and destinies. They are subject to the authoritarian and sometimes whimsical decisions of the white power structure. Both plantation and ghetto were created by those who had power both to confine those who had no power and to perpetuate their powerlessness. "The problem of transforming the ghetto is, therefore, a problem of power—a confrontation between the forces of power demanding change and the forces of power dedicated to preserving the status quo." [22]

For whites, the status quo must be maintained because blacks have always been seen, history tells us, as a contagion. The European social policy of colonization, slavery in the American South, Jim Crow, de jure and de facto segregation, and the miscegenation laws were just the most obvious ways blacks were to be kept separate from whites. Enclosing blacks in urban ghettos is in good form with the long standing European social policy of culturally and physically rejecting blacks. Whites feel justified in this behavior because to them being black is perceived as an infectious disease. Take this comment by Paul Jacobs, a liberal and a former civil rights activist. "The spittle sprayed against my face. I spun around, astounded, and saw no one except a tall young Negro, walking rapidly alongside me. It was he who had spat at me, I realized, and instantly I was flooded with anger, fright, an insane worry that his spittle was diseased, and then shame at the thought of such a disgusting fear." [23]

And what is done with a disease? It is isolated, contained, anesthetized, and killed when possible. It is this blackness that can wipe out whiteness if unrestrained, uncontrolled intermarrying were allowed between the two groups. Mixed marriages always produce black children. The people in the ghettos know that the whites perceive their blackness as being a disease. So, they have tried to look white by straightening their hair, lightening their skins, wearing outlandish colored clothing, adopting white mannerisms. But this has engendered a kind of schizophrenic self-hate. "Black is beautiful" did not stem the tide. It only strengthened the schizophrenia.

Human beings tend to fear disease because it is still very much a mystery to them. They do not like to be near anything that is judged diseased, and they will cringe at the thought of touching a diseased element. In America we have institutions for the purpose of controlling communicable diseases. From the point of view of whites, the ghetto is one of those institutions.

As a social institution, the role of the ghetto in the American social structure is largely determined by the dictates of the society as a whole. However, the ghetto does have a dynamic of its own that can have its influence on the overall social structure, i.e., the ghetto activism of the sixties. Police power is being used in the ghetto to prevent such influences. Therefore, the role of the police in the ghetto is that of an amalgam of the dictates of the American social structure and the dynamics of the ghetto.

In individual terms, it is these social and psychological forces which socialize the police officer to the role he must play on the beat in the ghetto. This is a process of secondary socialization, and, as we shall see, it is one of the more manipulative and potent social tools of modern America.

SOCIALIZATION

It is the purpose of this book to discuss the role of the police in the ghetto, and that point should not be forgotten during the early developmental stages of this essay. It is my intention to use the first three chapters of this book to lay the groundworks for a full discussion in chapter 4 of the police role(s) in the ghetto. In the first chapter, the reader was given an introduction to some of the more potent social forces that are at work in shaping the overall behavior of the police in the ghetto today. In this second chapter, we will look at the process one goes through to become a police officer; which is to say, we will consider the process used to recruit civilians to the force and the initial socialization of the aspiring neophyte within the police department.

Who is recruited for the police force and how he is trained is important to this analysis because I would maintain that the personal backgrounds of the individuals selected for police work, the training they receive, and their overall orientation into a police subculture tends to direct the attention of police officers to the ghetto; or, to put it differently, and perhaps a bit more accurately, the attention of police officers is directed towards the negative, sociocultural symbols the ghetto and black people in general represent in this society.

For example, the police represent law and order, and the ghetto is understood to be a community of institutionalized deviancy and crime. As a consequence, the police are naturally attracted to the ghetto community because of its deviancy and crime, and moreover they are disposed to relating to the ghetto as an adversary in both real and symbolic terms. Further, I would stress the fact that because of the events of the 1960s, ghetto activism, and the rise of the criminal justice ideology, there is now in existence a symbiotic relationship, and maybe this has always been the case, between the police and the ghetto. More than ever before, these two institutions have become dependent social forces.

As an illustration, so-called black radicals in the 1960s would point out that the presence of white, armed policemen in the ghetto was an indication that blacks were powerless and an oppressed people. "Throw out the pigs!" was their cry, and it was as much a call for black solidarity as it was a call for blacks to struggle against white domination of their community. To be sure, "Throw out the pigs!" did help the Black Panthers recruit members, but it also helped in getting blacks appointed to the police force and assigned to the ghetto.

At the same time, white police officers stress the dangers of working in the ghetto—how powerless and threatened the cop on the beat feels when he has to work in a community which does not support him. And one should not forget, these same policemen will remind us, that a "Black Liberation Army" is out there in the asphalt jungle dedicated to killing the pigs. In New York City, the Patrolman's Benevolent Association (PBA) frequently used the specter of ghetto danger as a backdrop in its negotiations with the city for more men and higher pay for police officers, and this same PBA exploited the ghetto dangers theme expertly in a successful effort in 1968 to defeat a proposed civilian review board.

Let us now look at the induction and indoctrination process that turns civilians into police officers, and later in this chapter we will see how this process is intimately related to the ghetto in both real and symbolic terms.

BECOMING A COP

Probably every American child has played cops and robbers at one time or another, in one form or another. From this game, at a very early age, we learn that the world is filled with good guys and bad guys. Once our young minds have grasped this symbolic reality, we readily accept the fact that it is always the bad guys who are tremendously aggressive and willfully predatory. They want to take what does not belong to them, and it is the job of the good guys to prevent this. It is the tried and true scenerio of the white hats versus the black hats, a view of the social world that is reinforced endlessly by motion pictures, TV, and books. From our "bang-bang" games and from the media messages, we learn to respect the cops as the good guys, just because they are cops. Even when there is bad-mouthing of the police, like that of the Serpico affair in New York City, or the findings that came out of the Knapp Commission (a commission empaneled to investigate corruption in the New York City Police Department), we will still tend to maintain a positive attitude about the police.

In the same way that we played our childhood games of cops and robbers, we like to believe that the chief function of the police is to catch criminals. This is also the way police personnel tend to see themselves. Moreover, the basic training of police officers is intended to give them a view of themselves as crook catchers and crime fighters. This crook catching image alone makes for a powerful bond between the police and the ghetto. The reason: most crooks, or committers of crime, are thought to be in the ghetto. The good guys always gravitate to where the bad guys are. This relationship has its own kind of symbiosis.

Playing the game of cops and robbers, by children or adults, bespeaks of our cultural beliefs in the inevitability of struggle between different social groups. The good guys against the bad guys presents us with an image of competing sides in a social contest. It is nature's way of producing superior people, the myths of Western history tell us. The asphalt cowboys against the ghetto crooks is just the most recent edition of an ongoing, long playing social process.

However, as is the case with human societies, myth must inevitably merge with reality. So then, we have the FBI statistics for major crimes that addresses itself to real acts of robbery, rape, murder and so on, and it is the police personnel who must put their real bodies on the line in the real struggle between the good guys and the bad guys. The rest of us participate symbolically in the contest through motion pictures, TV, books, and even through organized professional sports, most notably football.

Most of us participate in the contest only symbolically because we do not have what it takes to be one of the real good guys. It takes a special kind of person to be a police officer; that is to say, a person who is willing to lay his body on the line. It takes a person with a strong sense of duty and responsibility to the social order. Such a person is also likely to have strong beliefs in the purposefulness of life and the existence of a higher authority that shapes and directs most human experiences. These attitudes are frequently reflected in religious beliefs, among others, and the following general profile of a police recruit in New York City indicates this.

A young man who joins the police force is likely to be about twenty-four or twenty-five and of average intelligence. He has most likely worked at some sort of middle-class job before entering the police service for a year or two. "However, a more meaningful indicator of his place on the socioeconomic scale is his background, which is likely to have been a low to medium income, lower-middle working class family imbued with the Protestant work ethic [the belief in the Calvinistic theory that hard work and dedication to duty are the surest means through which to achieve both success and salvation] ."[1]

It is no accident that so many men with the above stated backgrounds find their way into police work. On one account, their background makes them suitable to the work, and on the other, this type of person is sought after by police departments. The choice of individuals to be inducted into the force is greatly influenced by the implicit meaning of police work in our society, and this meaning is an expression of the underlying values of our system that police power fundamentally serves. A further look at the above profile gives us indication of this.

The background of a police recruit will tend to encourage a certain ethnocentricity and bias, having both economic and social foundations, against minority groups in general, and blacks in particular. Also, it will encourage a physical rather than a verbal method of resolving conflicts. A policeman with such a background will tend to communicate with his clientele in an authoritarian and paternalistic manner and would assume that citizens could not be expected to be compliant without discipline and control. He is likely to be preoccupied with such matters as verifying his masculinity and maintaining his self-respect when challenged.

What makes our young recruit in question gravitate towards police work? "Until recently, there was a widespread feeling among sociologists and others that policemen were a self-selected group, attracted to an authoritarian profession by deep-rooted personality needs." [2] But today the belief is that most young men join the police force for security reasons; that is, financial security, say in terms of a pension at the end of twenty years of service. We are asked to believe that the policeman is not a violence-loving, authoritarian personality.

The argument goes: Yes, the police officer affects a certain posture, but he is no more prone to violence and possibly is a less authoritarian person than others who were raised and educated as he was. He has come to be a cop primarily for security reasons. "Although he is strong and athletic, he is not what you would call an adventurous or devil-may-care fellow. On the contrary he is a cautious and conservative man, both in his politics and in his moral nature." [3]

Academic researchers are no longer seeing the policeman as representing the "Cossack" stratum of society. However, the new image they are presenting of the policeman is that of an insecure, rigid personality who seeks his identity largely through compliance with authority. This would seem to make him, by nature, a defender of the status quo.

Referring to our young recruit in question once again: he is not likely to feel any need to alter the status quo; rather, he sees himself as the defender of the status quo. Political and moral challenges to authority seem to him at best antisocial and at worst treasonous. This is quite a logical attitude for him because *he* does not confront authority, he merely obeys it. To be sure, this is a critical component of his identity. He is an obedient person.

As defenders of the status quo, it was very easy for the police in the 1960s to see the ghetto activism as a threat to society. In many ways, there was not an ounce of difference to the police between the civil rights marchers and the Black Panthers. They were all trying to change the system. They all defied the law, and to that degree they were crooks, an evil force that needed to be treated viciously. To policemen from working-class backgrounds, "black-skinned activists and youthful protestors are the embodiment of everything that is alien, evil, and destructive of the American social system. Militant youths and black militants are perceived not only as un-American, but also nonhuman. Ruled out of the human race, they become nonpersons and therefore deserving of intense attack, as one would attack a rattlesnake."[4]

Police recruitment practices seek out young men who have compliant, insecure personalities. Frequently, they are young men who have tried their hands at other jobs, failed at them, or found those other job pursuits uninteresting and wanting. These young men turn to the civil service as a last chance at a good job that might offer them the opportunity for a middle-class way of life. These are young men with generally low career aspirations, and a desire for a conventional kind of lifestyle.

The recruitment practices of the police are the initial steps in the socialization of the neophyte into the world of being a cop. After passing a written intelligence examination, an applicant must pass a character reference which will be more difficult for him than the written test. Usually 50 percent of the applicants in New York City who pass the written test are eliminated during the character reference phase when something unfavorable is turned up in their background.

Some sophisticated candidates, who are aware of the character reference phase, begin their adjustment to the demands of their new career immediately after they are notified that they have passed the written examination. Looking towards the visit of a police department investigator, whose guiding principle is, "Any and every doubt must be resolved in favor of the department," they may dispose of books that might be considered too radical and drop friends with unsavory reputations. It is the principle of guilt by association that can be used to establish a case against an applicant, and there is little chance of redress for a candidate. The candidate will have to be "clean as a hound's tooth" to survive the character reference phase.

The police recruit is screened for any unconventional behavior, and if he passes the screening he has a right to feel proud of himself. Unfortunately, it probably also makes him feel as though he is morally superior to most of the people in society. This further means that he is already seeing himself apart from the public he will have to serve. Indeed, he is already beginning to look down on them. He is not to be their public servant; they are to serve his public ends.

The ties that bind the rookie cop to the civilian world are stripped away when he reaches the police academy. In secret and isolation he is taught the fundamentals of his job. However, the job training itself is secondary to the emotional impact of the experience on the rookie. The police academy is a "total institution" that "strips and mortifies" the recruit. "The stripping and mortification accelerate rapidly. Each neophyte proudly, albeit nervously, accepts the visible insignia of his new office: uniform, revolver, nightstick, and shield. Each of these symbols entails a continuous responsibility, which constantly reminds the recruit of his new role—a role that soon comes to dominate his personality."[5]

At the academy, the police recruit is required to disgorge himself from a social past while being absorbed into a social future. The present status of being a rookie recruit is ignored as much as possible, except as the brunt of ribbing and joking by the older members of the department. The police recruit at the academy is the lowest form of police life, similar to that of the ninety-day wonders, the second lieutenants in the army. He, the police recruit, is made to feel like nothing, but at the same time the insignia of police work, the badge, the gun, the nightstick are offered to the recruit as the means for him to redeem his self-respect and indeed his masculinity.

The training the policeman gets, which is very military in character and procedures, is designed to make the recruit as proficient as possible in a short period of time in the uses of the tools of his trade, the gun and the nightstick for example, and, to be sure, his physical body. The training is oriented towards the development of skills, skills to resolve conflicts in a physical manner rather than a verbal one.

The major emphasis of the curriculum content of police training academies is definitely on bodily skills. The content exhibits little evidence of practice in problem solving, learning the wise use of discretion, or learning the role of the police in society. It would seem obvious that more important to the police officer than repressive know how is the need to understand "the legal issues involved in his everyday work, the nature of the social problems he constantly encounters, and the psychology of those people whose attitudes toward law are different from his." From the President's Commission on Law Enforcement and Administration of Justice, we learn that the training focuses almost entirely on the apprehension and prosecution of criminals. "What a policeman does, or should do, instead of making an arrest, is rarely discussed. The peacekeeping and service activities which consume the majority of police time, receive too little consideration."

The learning process at the academy is wrapped in protocol and ceremony. The neophyte is confronted with a series of rites of passage that are used to give meaning to the progress being made by a recruit. Handshakes, a pat on the back or behind, standing at attention, a snappy salute or click of the heels all deepen and help to personalize the metamorphosis that is taking place. It is a new social environment for the recruit, where ritualized group responses tend to negate the individual self-presence, and indeed where individuality and the loner posture are scorned and put down.

The academy is a bridge, a gateway between two worlds. The only way to make the crossover is as a member of the group, by committing oneself to the fraternal order of the police. The training at the academy has shown the recruit his manner of deference to this order. The manner is internalized and readily becomes unconscious. One learns to do what he has to as a matter of doing the right thing. The right of individual purpose and initiative has been eroded in favor of the fraternal order.

The recruit comes to the academy with a great deal of idealism about the career he is going to assume. But just as his individual sense of purpose and initiative is eroded so is his idealism. At the start of his training, the police recruit has the tendency to hear only what he wants to hear, the good reasons why he has joined the force. But after a time

the alert student begins to realize that the professional atmosphere that surrounds him is partly a sham. This intuition may arise from the innuendos of his instructor; more often it is the result of the demeaning restrictions imposed upon his private life. In class he is taught that his exalted status as a policeman and peace officer endows him with tremendous power and responsibility. Outside of class the department indicates in many ways that it does not trust the young probationer. It sets a curfew for him; it declares stores where liquor is sold "off-limits." The recruit measures this treatment against the frequent appeals to him to conduct himself like a professional. Doubt assails him.[6]

The newness of every endeavor we encounter is expected to wear off after a time, but for the rookie policeman it is said that he is so shocked by the real world of police work intruding on his idealism that he develops a severe case of cynicism and suspiciousness very early in his career. One might readily ask why these young men are so shocked when they are faced with reality.

What the rookie cop experiences is a painful process of discovering that the beliefs and virtues he was taught to respect do not, in fact, reflect the reality of the world around him. Most people come to this awareness during adolescence. But Dr. Martin Symonds, resident consultant psychiatrist of the Medi-Unit of the New York City Police Department, himself a former policeman, notes that cops are typically people who "seem to have sidestepped the adolescent process and have gone from childhood directly to adulthood." This is to say that they seem to have muted or suppressed altogether the period of rebelliousness and questioning of authority. "These young men are idealistic," Symonds points out, "and have preserved an attitude toward authority that is one of respect, awe, and sometimes reverence."

Once the rookie cop leaves the academy, he is likely to run into another kind of cynicism almost immediately, probably on his very first day in the precinct. The older police officers are likely to tell him to forget everything he learned at the academy. "It is no use to you on the streets." Now the rookie begins to learn what it really means to be a cop. He learns this through a process that combines experiential learning and informal socialization. The two parts of the combination play off each other, and there are certain positive aspects to it. But, unfortunately, the negative components outweigh the positive.

To begin with, the informal socialization consists by and large of repudiating the formal training the rookie has only recently received. "You can't believe what they tell you at the academy. That's not the way it's done." The rookie may first refuse to accept this coaching, but since the neophyte must work with some older officer during his probationary period and that same older officer will have much to do with evaluating the neophyte's behavior, the young officer is likely to follow the guidelines laid down by his senior partner. Further, since police work is done on the two party, partner system, it is the older cop who decides if the younger cop is working out as a partner. If he is not working out and the older partner tells this to the other officers in the precinct, the other officers know that this particular rookie is not going along with the informal rules of the game. With pressure from most of the older officers, it does not take too long before the younger cop usually falls into line.

In falling into line the young police officer becomes prone to the syndrome of characteristics that have come to be associated very closely with the police profession: secrecy, defensiveness, and cynicism. Yet, there is another fact of the real world that is even more devastating to the idealism of the rookie cop, and there is nothing in his academy experience that prepares him for it. This is something that hits directly at the neophyte's self-image. Being a cop is a source of pride to him, he wants to be respected for it, for being the embodiment of law and order. But, as he emerges in the real world, he is not acclaimed; instead, he is criticized.

Moreover, he is taunted and scorned, and there is nothing a typical police officer dislikes so much as being criticized. "It upsets him. It makes him extremely defensive. In some cases he is not as concerned as he should be to be blameless, but in all cases he is more than normally concerned to be thought blameless."

The idealism of a young police officer is very apt to become tarnished by the organization he must work in—known to the cop as "the department." Police departments of large urban cities are known to be notorious bureaucracies. It is all too easy for an officer to lose his bearings in the labyrinth of hierarchy, specialization, competitive examinations, red tape, promotion based on seniority, impersonality, rationality, rules and regulations, channels of communications, and massive files.[7]

Much of the development of the bureaucratic labyrinths of police departments comes about because of two significant reasons: 1) police organizations use up a great deal of their energies trying to detect crimes, and 2) police organizations spend a great deal of time churning out statistical reports. The result of this is that a police officer spends as much time trying to detect and anticipate criminal behavior, along with the filling out of reports, as he spends actually catching crooks.

It cannot be emphasized enough that so much energy of the police as an organization is devoted to mobilizing resources for awareness of transgressions. We have all seen the warning signs that a section of a highway is being patrolled with radar equipment, a warning intended to caution and restrain potential violators by suggesting an extensive ambit of police awareness of violations. We are also very familiar with other technological and structural devices employed by police to learn of transgression. "Crimes of vice, for example, typically have no citizen complainants. The man who uses heroin, smokes marijuana, bets on a football game, or patronizes a prostitute does not complain to the police that someone has sold him narcotics, taken his bet, or has offered to go to bed with him for a fee. In order to enforce these laws police must develop an information system."[8]

A modern, big city police department is dedicated to churning out statistical reports. It is one of the main ways the department attempts to counter adverse criticism, defend itself, and in effect justify its existence. The need for statistics also serves as a reason for policemen to fill out the report records, even though the majority of officers really hate to do so. They are also used to signify accomplishment and action within the precinct and within the department that can give a picture to the public of an active, dynamic force working hard to prevent crime. This view may be totally inaccurate, but it can make the police officers feel better in knowing that the public is getting a good picture of them.

Relying upon statistics is the lifeblood of police organizations. For that reason, a great deal of time is spent grinding out the numbers: statistical reports of arrests, summonses, warnings, convictions, ambulance calls, fatalities.

Each case is transformed into a number and reported wherever possible in a manner that enhances the glory of the department. The contemporary trend to seek a cure for every personal problem in "analysis" has invaded the police bureaucracy. But whereas a patient in psychoanalysis supplies data by a stream of consciousness, it is the never-ending stream of statistics that symbolizes police case histories. The analysis unit is the main arm of defense in the struggle of the department to justify itself.[9]

When statistics are used to justify the existence of the organization in total, and in accordance with specific functions, it usually works in tandem with a process of over rationalization of departmental functions. This can be seen in exorbitant specialization that develops in police departments according to rank, function, union seniority, type of crime, tour of duty, uniform or undercover police roles, and so on. Also, this process has a way of rigidifying the command structure, and as the rookie cop is apt to find out, this can cause the policemen on the beat to back away from taking the initiative in making decisions. Instead, the line officer would rather rely upon a "rule-book mentality" that anticipates what commanders want rather than what the situation requires.

The rookie patrolman will learn that, at least in part, guiding one's hand by a rule-book mentality is an important way for the cop on the beat "to cover his ass." Police bureaucracies develop administrative hardening of the arteries in part because they are paramilitary in character, with a command structure that functions along hierarchical lines. It is a fact of military hierarchies that rank has its privileges. What commanders want is a matter of their privileges. Therefore, it is always best to give the commanders what they want, even when it seems inappropriate for the given situation.

The relationship of the department's command structure to the policeman of the beat is indirect. The relationship is therefore general and more at a distance. Commanders then develop a particularistic concern for the behavior of their men. It is not the police officer's overall behavior that will concern the commander, but the officer's behavior in a particular case.[10] Turning it around, this also means that normally the cop on the beat will relate to his commanders indirectly, through his sergeant and the chain of command, except when the cop is being singled out for particular recognition that favors or disfavors him. In any event, such meetings between commanders and subordinates are very rare. Consequently, most police officers think of their commanders as personally not giving a damn about them. When this realization comes to a neophyte, it can be a most painful awareness.

Nevertheless, the relationship that does exist between commanders and their men is very much defined for the latter by the extent to which they feel they are backed up (in the performance of their duty) by the former. Policemen feel very strongly about the fact that their commanders, right up to the police chief or commissioner, should back them up. But police officers do not always feel they get this support because they basically believe that their commanders don't give a hoot about them. This is very demoralizing to the cop, and the command structure's separation of commanders from their men serves to exacerbate the situation.

Of course, police commanders are aware of the fact that they are responsible for the morale of their men, but they also know that the nature of the policeman's role is such that it is continuously testing the relationship that has to support morale in the department. For instance, both commanders and their men know that the true facts about any incident, no matter what it involves, can rarely be established and that the standards governing the use of "necessary" force or "firm" language are inevitably vague, which is to say they are not standards at all. Whenever a contested situation develops, it is very likely that the commander wants to take the side of the police officer, and most frequently he does just that, but the choice is never an easy one for him.

To be sure, police commanders are caught in the middle of any contested situation between a member of the department and the public. He is caught because there are no clear-cut standards, no adequate rules, no reliable information, or sufficient resources that can be used to clarify the contested situation. Feeling out of touch because there are no firm solutions to the problem, commanders are likely to make imprudent public statements about contested situations. They may also rush to identify with their men by attacking (and enraging) those who fail to support the police and stir up trouble. Some commanders take the other side and try to soothe the community, and thus they enrage their own men by authenticating a fact that perhaps a police officer did overstep his bounds; or that perhaps it would be good to have a civilian review board. In truth, police commanders tend to develop two views on every situation, one for the public and one for the men in the department.

It is important to a police officer to feel that he is being backed up by his commanders, but at the same time he harbors a suspicion that he will not be. This is intensified by circumstances that lead the officer to conclude that the citizenry is indifferent or hostile to the police function. A patrolman inevitably faces hostility or a lack of cooperation from citizens. When this happens, he believes that he should get *more* backing from his superiors. But alas, he fears that he will get less because under these circumstances commanders must deal with more complaints and take such complaints more seriously as a result of the activities of organized pressure groups, especially civil rights and civil liberties groups, which put the heat on politicians who in turn are too timid to face them down. "The absence of agreed-upon standards for how the police should behave makes it hard for the patrolman, in his opinion, to do his job properly; the presence of many procedural rules makes it easy to penalize him for doing it, in somebody's opinion, improperly."[11]

It does not take very long in the career of a rookie cop before he becomes aware of the problems just mentioned. However he will find it difficult to adjust to such problems because it is the tendency among police officers to try to avoid dealing with them. Rather than solving problems, the police department as a whole, along with its individual members, tries to smooth things over. This comes about because among the police there is the strong belief that the way to solve problems, the all purpose solution, lies in esprit de corps; or to put it differently, blind chauvinism. Chauvinistic policemen are more concerned with the length of a man's sideburns than the quality of his work. As the urban police department has developed into a monolithic structure, there has been an increasing hue and cry for more "spit and polish."[12]

The maze, the labyrinth of modern organizational structures, causes workers to focus downward on matters directly in their purview and in their control. The need for self-expression, while at the same time extending a sense of control outwardly through one's immediate environment, can seemingly be satisfied through a commitment to esprit de corps. If nothing else, blind chauvinism seems to give officers the feeling of recapturing individual goals and initiatives from an organizational structure that absorbs them and turns them into organizational objectives.

Chauvinism among the police is very consistent with their general conservative natures, and it is reflected in their general attitudes toward crime. Police officers tend to think that crime should be suppressed by whatever means necessary. "Many police officers believe that the Constitution and civil liberties serve only to thwart their efforts. The work of William Vega indicated that most police officers see crime as the response of the individual, not associated with his environment. This value system of police conservatives enables them to dissociate the acts of individuals from society. Even well-read moderates find this value system difficult to accept."[13]

While this value system is challengable, it is uniquely suited to serve America's police. There is a psychology in it that expresses the one-to-one, the good guy versus the bad guy, rugged individualism, and the adversary state that exists between the police and the public they serve. Such a psychology just happens, as well, to be very consistent with the backgrounds of most police officers, in that such backgrounds tend to encourage a physical rather than a verbal method of resolving conflicts.

Conservatism, apart from the individual psychology, is also interwoven into the bureaucratic structure that is the police department. This is clearly exampled by the tendency of police departments to run on a system of management by abdication (MBA).

This consists of rule-oriented management personnel who attempt to implement change through fiat while simultaneously abdicating responsibility for it. An MBA organization is rule-oriented as opposed to goal-oriented and responsibility for service is difficult to identify because the emphasis is on procedure as opposed to results. The vast majority of police organizations are structured along paramilitary lines of command and control. This approach requires specialization and the development of functional responsibilities which facilitates management by abdication.[14]

MBA practices are enhanced by the very nature of the job the big city police department is called upon to do, policing of a city of millions of people; as well as by the nature of shared responsibility for police service on the streets. To begin with, responsibility for providing police service in specific geographic areas of a city is most difficult to determine in highly specialized, big city police departments. The police service is segmented and there are overlapping responsibilities. This is a consequence of the fact that a city is divided up into precincts, with each such division having its own commanders, lieutenants and a captain. Then, there are the special squads and details like narco, bunco, SWAT, homicide, which may be under the control of bureau chiefs. The generalist, that is the uniformed officer on patrol, and the technicians from the specialized squads are all out there on the street together. Whereas the police officer may want to idolize himself as going one on-one with the crooks, that view is far from the truth.

Crime fighting in modern urban society is done by crime control teams in which the policeman on the beat is but one part, if he is a part of it at all. Frequently, the rookie cop will find himself excluded from any meaningful role in crime control. He is likely to be given the "shit details" —getting into an apartment of a very ripe stiff (a badly decomposed body), taking the sick and begotten to hospitals or other social service shelters, watching guard over traffic in a fire zone. There are no thrilling one-on-one confrontations in these situations, just as there are few such moments in a system of crime control teams. The specific problem here is that team operations have a way of stifling individual initiative, and it is this initiative, this one-on-one, this rugged individualism, that is likely to be the centerpiece to many a young cop's self-image.

Within the police department itself, there is much confusion about what should be the police role. Policemen have not been trained to differentiate their responses to meet changing requirements. Their roles are products of a rule-oriented structure. Consequently, this has led police officers to see themselves as constantly being confronted with demands from the community for varying types of service which they have not been trained to handle. This has resulted in a situation where police officers feel threatened by the changing demands of the community.

The status of police work is based upon law enforcement; the enforcement of the law has a certain aura of glamour associated with it. To be a public servant is to be less than an enforcer. Yet, police officers are confronted with a paradox since the community demands more service than law enforcement. Does a police officer enforce laws or provide service to the community? Since individual police officers have no direct responsibility to the community, and little or no contact with the political process, they are, in effect, free agents.[15]

It is quite true that policemen feel disconnected, disassociated, and floating free from the community life around them, both in their on the beat community and the community where they live. The reasons for this are many as indicated by much of what has already been said in this chapter. Nevertheless, one of the main reasons why the police officer becomes isolated has to do with the fact that in the public's eye the policeman embodies and personifies the law. It does not matter whether he is in or out of uniform, the policeman is empowered to enforce the law. This enforcement may require him to use a gun, and to the extent that he has the right to use a gun when necessary, he is a symbol of authority. And, to put it more accurately, he is much more than a symbol. Indeed, the policeman is an agent, an agent who embodies the sovereign right of the state to take lives.

Some experts in the police field have concluded that because the police are floating free as a group from the community life around them they have come to constitute, in and of themselves, a minority subculture. It is to be well understood that to say that any group constitutes a subculture is to be able to point to certain important and distinctive features that set it apart from other subcultures or from society at large. Most often the term is used to describe ethnic and religious groups. We are able to readily recognize that the Amish, Orthodox Jews, Mexican Americans and many other similar groups are subcultures; that is to say, little islands of identity with unique customs, histories, outlooks, and ideals, afloat in the larger American cultural sea.

The idea of subculture is also used to describe groups who are organized around the violation of laws or norms. Groups like homosexuals, prostitutes, addicts, and the like. The special worlds of these groups are maintained through group solidarity, the sense of loyalty and belonging that inspires individual members and limited, circumscribed interaction with outsiders.

Even more important than what a subculture is, is the fact that its existence bespeaks of a unique kind of socialization that its members have had to experience in order to formulate their group. Undoubtedly, these are secondary socialization processes, but this in no way negates the powerful effect the processes have had on individual personalities. Also, it needs to be pointed out that the identities of the people in these sub-cultures are just as much a result of what society thinks of them, as of what they may think of themselves.

Subcultures, in a manner of speaking, can also be seen as public-private fraternal groups that demand recognition from the larger culture on the one hand, while striving mightily to maintain their exclusiveness on the other. However, in order to maintain their exclusiveness they must in the process foster their own isolation.

The police are not only different from most of the rest of us in terms of their conceptions about the world, but like nuns and hippies they have a distinctive garb which sets them apart. Furthermore, like nuns, the police are virtually cloistered from the world except when performing their occupational duties (during which time they admittedly mainly view an odd portion of life).[16]

There are many different reasons why police find themselves in social isolation, and along with what has already been mentioned on the subject we need to speak more on it because it is such an important factor of police behavior. For example, Skolnick points out that policemen are required to enforce laws that represent puritanical morality like prohibit ing drunkenness and regulating traffic laws.

In these situations the policeman directs the citizenry, whose typical response denies recognition of his authority, and stresses his obligation to respond to danger. The kind of man who responds well to danger, how-ever, does not normally subscribe to codes of puritanical morality. As a result, the policeman is unusually liable to the charge of hypocrisy. That the whole civilian world is an audience for the policeman further promotes police isolation and, in consequence, solidarity.[17]

Another way of understanding Skolnick's point is this: because the police must enforce laws that impinge on common social and leisure activities of the community, the police who also engage in the same activities try to protect themselves by segregating their social lives out of sight of ordinary citizens. In practically every large American city there are police clubs which are maintained by the local police protective, fraternal, or benevolent organization. These are private clubs with restricted memberships to police and those individuals whose activities bring them into the floating world of the police. Here the police can be as rowdy, as loud, and get as drunk as they like, and it is all kept among themselves.

The police also tend to segregate their other organizational affiliations within a special police-dominated world. Consequently, you have special police posts of veterans and military groups, masonic lodges only for police, special religious groups for police, shooting clubs, and so on. What this all means is that the police are further set apart from the civilian world because their off-duty time is not spent with nonpolicemen, and thus this facilitates the extent to which the special features of their occupation produces a distinctive outlook and subculture.

Solidarity among the police has many sources. One source lies in the fact that the police experience a shared sense of danger and must rely upon one another for protection. It is in the nature of teamwork, cooperation, mutual responsibility—in short, to help your buddy and look after him—that is extraordinarily high among policemen. Janowitz has commented on military men that "any profession which is continually preoccupied with the threat of danger requires a strong sense of solidarity if it is to operate effectively." At the same time, police work is not nearly so dangerous as policemen think it is, but what they think is all that matters for creating solidarity.

Police are trained to think of themselves as crook catchers and sleuths. This view of oneself breeds suspicion. Suspicion is an institutionalized characteristic of the police role. This is another source of segregation and solidarity for the police. Nonpolice persons tend to feel uncomfortable around police because of the police's suspicious nature. Of course, when only policemen are together this characteristic of their role does not bother them.

And too, the social isolation of the police is aided and abetted by the work schedules of the police. They work around the clock, on shifting tours of duty. On two out of three tours they are working when most people are not. And now that most policemen travel a beat in a patrol car, they no longer have the contact they used to with the people on the streets. Technology has helped to deepen the policeman's isolation.

Isolation goes hand in hand with subculture designation, and the police qualify eminently for the first which further seems to have the habit of leading directly to the second. For the police, solidarity is the other side of isolation. The socialization of the cop calls for him to develop a strong sense of solidarity, and he will do this at the risk of cutting off his ties with the civilian world. To be in the public view as a fact of the garb one must wear, but at the same time trying to shield oneself from it, does create, in the words of Niederhoffer and Blumberg, "the ambivalent force."

Ambivalence can be very frustrating. To be sure, frustration seems to be endemic to the policeman's role, along with the stress that comes with it. But most important, the system that the policeman works in, the organizational structure, the ambience of the solidarity to isolation syndrome, its subculture nature, and so on, seems to be designed and constituted to produce frustration. Perhaps it can be said that the policeman works in a dysfunctional system. This notion seems to be exampled in a recent study that was made of the New York City Police Department.

The study found that there was a "pervasive" frustration, on the part of line and superior officers, with existing conditions in the New York City Police Department. This frustration was preventing the department from operating at maximum efficiency. The main cause for this frustration, says the study, is police officers' dissatisfaction with such conditions as the current work schedules that mandate weekly rotation of tours, the department's reward and recognition systems, and the poor public image of the department, including "the seemingly derogatory media exposure."

A major dissatisfaction among the officers was the department's work schedule or chart. The chart called for an officer to perform a set of five "day" tours (8 a.m. to 4 p.m.), followed by a set of five "midnights" (midnight to 8 a.m.), and then five "4 to 12's" (4 p.m. to midnight) "Before this chart went into effect, precinct commanders had the authority to schedule volunteers to work steady hours, without rotation, provided the commander could maintain minimum manpower levels around the clock. One reason for the new chart reportedly was that some precincts were found to be undermanned on some tours."

The study said that the mandated tour rotation increased physical, mental, and emotional stress. Many police officers, the report continued, viewed the new chart as an attempt by the police administration to get even with the Patrolman's Benevolent Association because the union had fought the administration over salary, working conditions, and other issues.

The reward system in the department was especially disturbing to the officers. Those who were interviewed made such comments as: "Recognition is given only in the form of criticism," "Slackers are treated the same as stars," "Who wants another medal—you have to fill out forms and then they're thrown at you," and "We're treated like numbers."

As for the department's public image, the report said that public misconceptions—fed by police dramas on television—"contribute to the feelings of dissatisfaction, depression, and frustration" that are shared by many officers. "The officer on television is invariably successful," the report noted, "and the public expects the same success from the officer on the street." [18]

A dysfunctional system is an incomplete system, a system where the people involved are always feeling short changed, abused, and maligned. It is a system of many *starts* and many *finishes*, but frequently there are few connections between the two. Therefore, decisions can be made to change the work schedule without any thought being given to consultations with police officers and commanders who would be affected directly by the change, and beyond any doubt, criticism is a one-sided, incomplete form of recognition.

The rookie cop is socialized piecemeal into this dysfunctional system. If he had to take it all in at one shot it is very likely his personality would crumble. It is over the months and years that the policeman learns to build up his tolerance to the frustrations and cynicism that knit the norms of his job together. However, without knowing it he has become a polished social instrument that has been stretched like the bow that holds the arrow.

THE GHETTO AS HIDDEN ADVERSARY

Having now discussed the induction and indoctrination of the civilian into the police lifestyle and subculture, we will now consider the manner in which this process relates to the ghetto.

The affinity of the police to the ghetto actually has its beginnings in the personal backgrounds of individual officers, and to the degree that all of us as kids have played cops and robbers, we all have had this childhood initiation: the white hats versus the black hats. We didn't know it then but we were learning our basic color symbols for good and evil, for the good guy cops and the bad guy robbers, and by the time we have reached adulthood, the symbols have been reinforced thousands and thousands of times.

All Americans grow up with the knowledge that our society accepts white people as being socially and humanly better than black people. In this view, compared to blacks, white people are the eternal good guys, the superior people, who have a moral obligation to fight the bad guys wherever they are found. Every white person is not required to do his own fighting today. Our society has agents, the police, who are paid to do it for them. The police are our superheroes, our real life Batmans and Spidermans, who are willing to lay it all on the line to protect the common good. They travel to the enemy's lair to fight him, one-to-one on his own turf. They travel into the dark ghetto, knowing that it is crawling with bad guys, the jungle bunnies who are ready to swipe them down at a moment's notice. But the police are willing to endanger themselves because they have in their ranks some of this society's best people. For New Yorkers they are "New York's Finest!"

These men are willing to lay it all on the line. They are men who have a strong sense of social duty, and they dedicate their vocation to serving it. This dedication is backed by a strong Protestant work ethic which says that success and salvation will be yours through hard work. This Calvinist ideology also holds that man's work on earth is really work that is being done for God, and of all the work that people can do for God, rooting out evil specifically is the most praiseworthy. And where is evil, in the form of deviancy and crime, most prevalent in our society? In the ghetto. So, behind their shields, the policemen have a bit of the Calvinist messenger in them that turns their heads routinely towards the ghetto.

The majority of policemen come from working-class backgrounds. Working-class families are known to be very authoritarian and adult centered. Children from such families grow up having been very much controlled and dominated by their parents. Gordon Allport has written that families of this type, where the environment is suppressive, harsh, and critical, and where the parents' word is law, are likely to produce children who are predisposed to prejudice.

Allport reached his conclusion from the following analysis. He said that when parents give or withhold love in an absolute, arbitrary kind of manner, it forces the child to function in a highly sensitive state, one that keeps the child very frightened of their disapproval. At the same time, these dominating parents are shaping the child's conception of reality to such a degree that the child comes to accept a world of domination and authority as more correct than a world of equality and trust. The child grows up trying to find ways to relieve himself of his parents' domination and authority. One of the ways he learns to do this is not to question their right to make decisions for him. But, he may also come to fear and distrust his own impulses as a result because it is through the free expression of his impulses that he runs afoul of his parents' authority. In the end, says Allport, the child projects his shortcomings, the fear and distrust he has onto others, in particular onto strangers. It is easy for him to think of them as having evil designs and forbidden aims.[19]

People who are predisposed to prejudice for the reasons mentioned above are very likely to seek out systems and situations that will allow them to dominate others, like parents dominating their children, or any situation where the strong dominates the weak, and where the dominator's word is law. The ghetto is a perfect crucible for individuals of this stripe who are in a position to use some recognized, sanctioned authority. Policemen have such authority and they very likely have this type of predisposition to prejudice, and if we can believe James Baldwin, it all comes together and gets expressed for the policeman in the ghetto. Police officers tend to have an avowed interest and fascination in the ghetto beat, and once an officer has worked in a ghetto for any length of time he doesn't want to work in a nonghetto precinct.

Any person who grows up distrusting his own impulses is likely to lean towards the insecure side of his personality. While experts believe that most young men join the police force today for security reasons in terms of salary, job stability, and pension, the security these young men may actually be seeking is emotional security. Being a member of a highly visible, closely knit group like the police can help to stabilize insecure feelings, but at the same time such feelings can never be completely stabilized. Therefore, the individual feels that he must be continually establishing and reestablishing his connection and relationship to the group in the eyes of the public. Most simply, policemen can do this by fighting off challenges to their authority in the public domain. This can go from forcing a ticket on a motorist who feels he does not deserve it, to making roustabouting noisemakers retire from public places, to firing a gun at a suspect who refuses to stop running when commanded to do so.

With the exception of the latter case, the activities just described can and do happen in the normal course of duty for practically any policeman, but it is well known that the pace of police activities is greatly accelerated in the ghetto. There are many more chances in general to fight off challenges to police authority there. The people of the ghetto are likely to be more suspicious and questioning of police behavior, and their overall manner towards the police is more likely to be disrespectful than respectful. As Marlon Brando pointed out in the motion picture *Sayonara,* "There is such a thing as insolence through manner."

Generally speaking, policemen, by their own admission, are a group of borderline losers, they are men who have tried other pursuits, but they have failed in those endeavors. Eventually they turned to civil service for job and economic security. Apparently, many of these men, prior to joining the force, had lost faith in their own abilities to survive in the comparatively insecure job world outside of civil service. Yet, these same men with such poor self-images are then able to pass a rigid mental and physical examination, and an onerous character reference. They come through this feeling morally superior to most of the people in society, which is to say, that as losers they have now been made to feel like winners.

Having seen himself as a loser, the rookie cop can really enjoy the feeling of his success in having made it on the force, and he wants to continue feeling like a winner by being a good cop. Being a good cop to the novice means chasing down criminals, making arrests, "getting collars." At what station in the city will the officer have his best chance to be a good cop, a winning cop? Why, in the ghetto. As well, police officers want to see themselves in a positive light. It is a way of forgetting their loser image. Any criticism can be a reminder of those pre-police officer days. As a consequence, on these grounds alone, the policeman finds himself overly sensitive to criticism from any source, especially criticism from fellow officers.

The experience of recruits at the police academy, the secrecy of the training, its unrelatedness to a previous civilian lifestyle, its ritual nature, is the initial basis for the insulation the policeman develops to combat criticism. The academy experience gives the trainee the impression that the public should not be involved internally in police affairs. Later, this attitude is expanded to all police activities. This is one of the main reasons why the police find it so difficult to accept civilian review boards. They have been indoctrinated to believe that to allow civilian involvement in the internal operations of the police is practically to break a holy covenant. In this same way, to allow minorities on civilian review boards is therefore a sacrilege.

The academy experience also leaves the recruit feeling like a dominated child. The tentacles of academy time have dug into his private life—the off-limits establishments. By the time the rookie cop graduates from the academy, he feels like he has to bust out of the system of indoctrination and control. It is the only way he can redeem himself, recapture his lost self-respect and self-image. The indoctrination also makes it very clear that the way the rookie policeman can recapture his self-esteem is through the use of the nightstick, the gun, the policeman's recognized authority. Where can a novice policeman get that immediate busting out action he wants? In the ghetto. Further, for reasons already mentioned, police departments would like to assign more rookie cops to high crime districts and ghetto communities initially. But they are usually restricted in the number they can assign because the "old heads," who may have been in high crime precincts for many years, do not want to leave the precincts with the heavy action.

The training of the policeman is oriented to the development of skills, the skills in the use of physical force. This means he must know how to use the tools of his trade; the nightstick, blackjack, and gun. However, the most important tool that is being sharpened is the policeman himself. He is being trained as a law enforcement instrument. He is being trained to put his body on the line. He is being trained to use his body against criminals, and where are most of the criminals that would require him to put his body on the line? In the ghetto. This is especially true because the chief aspect of the policeman putting his body on the line lies not in his nightstick, blackjack, or gun, but rather in the fact that the policeman who patrols the ghetto is likely to be, and indeed society would prefer him to be, white. It is the color-good that must directly confront the color-bad; because it is the color-good that can directly intimidate the color-bad.

Much of the energies of the police department are taken up with attempts to detect crime through undercover work, a communications network, preventive patrols, and so on. As the ghetto is seen as a high crime area, a great deal of these energies are inevitably directed towards the ghetto. And as we have said, the police department spends a great deal of time churning out statistics that are used to justify its existence. Most of the data for these statistics, crime rates, the drug traffic, juvenile delinquency, and the like, have their origins in the ghetto. All of this is to say that the ghettos are very responsible for the character and operations of police departments in big city areas.

There are much less circuitous indications of the dependency of big city police departments on the ghetto. Without ghetto crime and the belief that the ghetto is a community of institutionalized deviancy, big city police departments would have a difficult time justifying their huge budgets which can run into the hundreds of millions of dollars. And the growth of police organizations into sprawling bureaucracies is only tangentially related to the increase in crime. That is to say, bureaucracies have not really grown as a result of the police increasing their capacity to fight crime.

Bureaucratic organizations tend to grow and expand as they seek greater efficiency. Efficiency may be gained, it is believed, through increased specialization of functions in terms of the organization's goals. Therefore, the organization will move for greater and greater specialization which in turn will require it to develop new systems, divisions, inner departments, and the like, and hire or create specialists to fill these positions. Thus, the organization must inevitably expand and grow. Because of the search for greater efficiency, the organization is attempting to bring more and more rationality into its functioning. This is called factoring.

It should be understood that organizations are problem-solving mechanisms that depend upon a factoring of the general goal into subgoals and these into subgoals, and so on, until concrete routines are reached. It is that the subgoals are allocated to organizational units and become the goals of those units. As a consequence, individuals in the units are not given the impossible task, therefore, of evaluating their every action in terms of the general goal of the organization, but only in terms of the particular subgoal allocated to their units. "The definition of the situation is sufficiently simplified to bring it within the rational capacity of the human mind. If the factoring is accurate, rationality in terms of each unit will be rationality in terms of the organization as a whole. In this way, bureaucratic organizations achieve rationality far beyond the capacity of any individual."[20]

In a bureaucracy factoring can occur at any time, but for a police organization, reports of increases in crimes can spur it on, and one can see this in terms of increased specialization. There develops the bunko squad, the vice squad, the narco squad, the special rape detail, among many others. The department expands and grows, but this does not mean that there are more crime fighters on the streets trying to prevent the occurrence of crime or catching criminals. The report of increasing crime gives the bureaucracy a reason to expand and grow, and the ghetto as a high crime area specifically inspires the growth. As growth and expansion can be seen as a reward for accomplishments or increased responsibilities, ghetto inspired factoring can be cited as an example of the good job the department is doing, and this rationalization can be used to help defend and protect the police department from criticism.

Police personnel can be very emotional about defending themselves because they believe that their efforts are being thwarted by the Constitution of the United States, the government, and the courts. The police feel that these social agents give too much respect to civil liberties. Since the 1954 school desegregation decision by the Supreme Court, the courts in general have tended to be more liberal in their concerns for the rights of suspects and defendants. The police saw this trend as benefiting primarily minority groups, in particular blacks. This gave them a reason to have a special animus towards blacks and their community. It was because of them, the blacks, that the courts were frustrating the police's efforts.

Now, let us shift our angle of analysis a little. So far in this section I have been attempting to show that the special characteristics of the police have a way of directing much of their attention, both overtly and covertly, towards the ghetto. However, there is an even more important reason, not yet mentioned, as to why the attention of the police is so taken up with the ghetto. Rodney Stark gives us our lead in. He says that the individual aspects of the police make up the totality of a minority subculture, and he goes on to say that the nature of the police subculture automatically puts the police at odds with other subcultures, certainly the black ghetto subculture.

Because of their unique position in the social system, the American police constitute a minority subculture and this is both a cause and a consequence of the estrangement the police feel from the rest of society. This police subculture especially conflicts with other subcultures that have interests, norms, and ideals different from those of the police and this conflict is exacerbated by the prejudice and fear that typically accompany such conflicts. It is not only the blacks, but other racial minorities as well that come into direct conflict with the police subculture, along with political and social dissenters, both students and adults. These conflicts can be fraught with reciprocal anger, hatred, violence, and fear.

The basis for Stark's conclusions flow from the findings of social scientists on racial and ethnic relations. It has been found that when two groups, such as the police and the blacks, differing on highly valued traits such as race, ethnicity, religion, language, customs, and differing on just a general social orientation, come into contact with one another, their conflicts tend to give rise to prejudice. They come to see one another in terms of invidious stereotypes and beliefs, which manifest suspicion, fear, and hostility.

Indeed, in a classic research study, the generation of such phenomena of prejudice was observed among arbitrarily selected groups of boys at a summer camp. When one or both groups feel that their own "ways" have a monopoly on virtue and legitimacy, the processes of prejudice are greatly encouraged. Obviously, the forms in which intergroup hostilities will manifest themselves depend upon the relative power of the two groups involved. When one group is disproportionately powerful it tends to discriminate against, repress, persecute, and otherwise victimize the less powerful. The less powerful tend to respond by symbolic aggression and by acts of defiance, rebellion, and harassment.[21]

If the analysis above is correct, along with the fact that the police are a subcultural group in conflict with other subcultures on important matters, then, says Stark, several predictions can follow. First, the police and the other relevant subcultures will, and do, manifest considerable prejudice, hostility, and fear towards one another. And second, it is to be expected that the prejudice and hostility will increase directly according to the extent to which the two groups come into contact with one another, and correlatively, that prejudice and hostility will be more common among individual members of the groups the more often they come into contact with each other.

Do these predictions bear empirical truth in the real world? Well, let us see. In writing the book *Nobody Knows My Name* (1962), James Baldwin characterized the police in the ghetto as an army of occupation. Not long after the comment was made, the country was rocked by a series of riots and gun battles. Ghetto residents and policemen were killed. During the latter years of the 1960s, the police in the ghetto were not so much an occupying force as they were counterinsurgency raiders: get in and out fast was the tactic. At this time, black rage had become generally focused on the police. Cries from the ghetto, like that of Watts, of "Get whitey" became more intense and gave way to the Black Panther call to "Off the pigs."

The police responded in kind. With a fear of black people, it was easy to openly express violent hostility and prejudice towards them. In Los Angeles, the police greeted each other with the old Lucky Strike slogan: LSMFT which they translate as "Let's shoot a mother fucker tonight." Many police officers called their nightsticks and riot batons "nigger knockers." This was not just all talk. Reports from cities around the country, including Detroit, San Francisco, Chicago, New York, Oakland, and Philadelphia indicated that police officers attacked or shot members of the black community, Black Panthers for instance, at offices, social events, at home in bed, and even in the halls of a courthouse.

Of course, police hatred and repression of black people is hardly new, and historically it has been mainly the police who enforced the cruel customs of racism. And surely, it was not only peculiar to Southern lawmen. Yes, we all know that police racism is not new, but recently something new has developed from it. This has made the relationship between the police and the ghetto more urgent and intense during the past decade. Whereas the police have long had their repressive way with black people, it has been only recently that the police have seemingly come to openly show fear of them. However, even the fear that the police have of blacks in the ghetto is in itself a drawing force that pulls the cop's attention towards that community. If you believe you have an enemy, you are likely to want to know what he is doing. And, for a policeman, there can be a certain excitement just in the knowledge that he is in the lion's den.

CHAPTER 3

INSTITUTIONAL ATTENDANTS

In the previous chapter we learned that elements in the personal backgrounds of police officers, the nature of police work, and the ensuing lifestyle of these individuals have the consequence of imbuing them with certain predispositions. There is little doubt that these predispositions help to shape the role of the police officer on the beat in the ghetto. But more than that, it is probably more correct to say that these predispositions are likely to be very deterministic in helping to shape the policeman's role in the ghetto. The stronger sentiment can be easily understood within the following context. If the police officer comes to the ghetto with the belief that the ghetto is filled with bad guys because it is a community of institutionalized deviancy and crime, then this is likely to be the basis for his interpretations of the actions and events that are to involve him.

Sociological studies in race and ethnic relations tell us that the whites' view of the ghetto is based on much more than the stereotype of the denigrated Negro. For whites in general, which takes in the posture and attitudes of the overwhelming majority of police, the ghetto materializes, if we may use the words of Robert K. Merton, as a self-fulfilling prophecy. This is to say that not only do whites see what they want to see in the ghetto, but also that their preconceptions will allow them to see very little else about the community. In the self-fulfilling prophecy process, one's perceptions, even though they may be wrong, take precedence over reality.

But the aforementioned point is only one side of the self-fulfilling prophecy phenomenon. As perception is taking precedence over reality, there is, and must be, an interplay between the perceptions that a policeman brings to the ghetto and the reality of what the ghetto truly is. This type of interacting process was described by Gunnar Myrdal in *An American Dilemma,* a process which he called the "principle of cumulation." Myrdal pointed out that while prejudice and discrimination keep the black low in standards of living, health, education, manners, and morals, this, in turn, gives support to white prejudice. White prejudice and black standards thus mutually "cause" each other . Such a static "accommodation" is, however, entirely accidental. "If either of the factors changes, this will cause a change in the other factor, too, and start a process of interaction where the change in one factor will continuously be supported by the reaction of the other factor." Gunnar Myrdal's commentary here is pointing out the fact that there has developed a certain general interdependence between the social factors in black-white relations, and I would suggest that this same type of interdependence has specifically developed between the police and the black urban ghetto.

Both Merton's and Myrdal's observations flow from a much more profound statement made by W. I. Thomas. Thomas said, "If we define a situation as real, it is real in its consequences." In this observation he is saying that perceptions can determine their own set of real outcomes, even if those perceptions are based upon false beliefs and/or error in judgments.

A concrete example of what Thomas is talking about can be seen in the following illustration. Two white policemen on patrol in a squad car are called to a scene of a robbery in progress. Upon their arrival, they observe a black man running away from the scene of the alleged robbery. They leave their squad car and give chase after the black man, removing their revolvers from their holsters as they run. The policemen shout at the man, telling him to stop, but the man does not do so immediately. However, after a chase of about a block the man does stop abruptly and turns to face the onrushing officers. As the man turns to face them, the two white police officers see that he has a gun in his hand. Without any further word of warning, both policemen fire at the suspect, striking him twice in the chest. The black man collapses on the sidewalk, dead from a shot through the heart. The policemen feel relieved. It was either him or them. They got off their shots first. However, when the two policemen examine the body for identification they discover that the black man is a police officer, a plainclothes detective.

This type of incident occurs all too frequently in big cities. The white policemen had assumed that a black man running away from the scene of a crime must be a criminal suspect. When the black man seemingly turned on them with a gun in his hand, that confirmed their suspicion. Firing their pistols at the man was a logical progression from their original definition of the situation. It would be very difficult to explain to the two white policemen that perhaps they had done something wrong, like over-reacting because of certain predispositions they may have towards blacks.

The predispositions that policemen bring with them to the ghetto are an unconscious form of labeling that colors their behavior, and this colored behavior can produce certain desired outcomes in the relationship between the police and the ghetto community. The incident just described is an example of police behavior that produces a certain desired outcome. We can understand it this way: The police see themselves as crook catchers. They arrived on a scene to see what they thought was a crook trying to escape. It was their job to stop him. The desired outcome in the first instance was to prevent the robbery, but if that was not possible then surely they had to catch the crook. When the suspect seemingly turned on them, the situation had evolved into its simplest form—the white hats against the black hat, and in the dramaturgy of American cultural life, the white hats are supposed to win. Win they did.

The preconceived notions of the police towards the ghetto greatly influences the pattern of their behavior. There are two prominent notions that most citizens become readily aware of once they have had serious contact with the police. Built into police action is the "must win" reflex, and the "I'm not taking any crap" attitude. The white hats are supposed to win, but they will not win if they take crap off of the crooks. This makes the policeman's behavior intensely personal, which means they go about their work in the ghetto with a strong feeling of "them and us." This attitude tends to cause the policeman to put even more stress on the racial and ethnic differences between himself and the people he may serve in the ghetto.

All of this means that the policeman comes to the ghetto predisposed to perform in certain ways at the behest of the larger society and the residents of the ghetto community. The police in the ghetto are respond-ing to many callings, some of which are very, very subtle indeed. To be sure, it is probably wrong to say that crime or the threat of crime, is the principal force shaping police behavior in the ghetto. It is nothing that specific. It is more likely to be the subliminal, sociocultural factors of race relations in America and the effect of self-fulfilling prophecy. We can be-come more aware of the main role of the police in the ghetto, along with its subsidiary, conjunctive aspects, by trying to understand the con-fluence of these sociocultural factors. Therefore we will now scrutinize some of the factors in preparation for a thorough discussion of the police role in the ghetto in the next chapter.

RULE ENFORCERS

In the first instance, the policeman appears in the ghetto as an agent—a societal agent of the established authority for law and order, the maintenance of the status quo, and so on. He comes to the ghetto specifically as an outsider whose presence in the ghetto is as that of a rule enforcer.[1] The people in the ghetto know that he is there to enforce rules that help perpetuate their deprived, ignominious existence in a society that has judged them to be social throwaways. The very sight of the policeman in the ghetto evokes fear, awe, excitement, and scorn. Policemen are to be despised because they are perceived as doing the society's dirty work.

In the immediate sense, the blue uniformed policeman can attract a "free-floating" animosity and enmity that exist in the ghetto among its residents for established authority, the status quo, and the rule enforcers in general. For the moment, the policeman walking on the street, in the passing patrol car, can become the object of pent up, festering hostilities that tend to reside in ghettoized people for those they consider to be their oppressors. The policeman helps to pull this kind of response from the people in the ghetto by the fact that he looks upon them suspiciously, a characteristic that is built into the behavior of the policeman. He is always looking for the bad guy.

Transferring this free-floating animosity and enmity to the police officer is a release mechanism for ghetto residents. It helps to relieve pent up frustrations, that, left without an object, seethe and more readily boil over into social eruption. We need not exaggerate the importance of this phenomenon, but at the same time, we should not minimize it. Where the police act only as recipient of this free-floating enmity, that is when they do not respond in kind to the penetrating, shooting stares, the slurring, condemning, ducking eyes, and even the open verbal abuse of "pig" or "motherfucking oppressors," the free-floating action can act as a "lid-cracking exercise" that helps to relieve the pressures for ghetto dwellers of being discriminated against as a way of life.

To better understand the lid-cracking exercise is to see it from the point of view of the police rather than oppressed blacks. When blacks in the ghetto express their free-floating enmity, they are venting their frustrations, that is pushing up the lid that holds the pressure on them. When the police allow this venting, without response, the pressure is somewhat relieved. However, when the police react to this venting, subtly or with force, their action is to force the lid of pressure back on tight and therefore disallowing a venting of frustrations. Of course this tends to be the response of the police, more often than not, because such venting can be interpreted as a questioning of their authority and as a rule enforcer challenges such as this are not expected to go unheeded. Rule enforcers are not supposed to take any crap from the minions. Not taking any crap, and the need to give a little crap, are ingredients that can lead to physical confrontation between police and ghetto residents. This was probably one of the chief underlying factors in the riots of the 1960s.

Social investigators like Rodney Stark and Tom Hayden have pointed out that the not taking any crap attitude among policemen is sometimes used as justification and license for official violence. Hayden gives a detailed picture of this in his book *Rebellion In Newark,* in which he exposes the anatomy of a riot. One of Hayden's main points is that the official violence of the police brought on a ghetto response which the police and the larger society then deemed a riot. Stark says that because the police are a subculture this automatically puts them at odds with the black subculture, or if you will, the ghetto and its residents.

Not "taking any shit off of the public" is extraordinarily important to policemen because as rule enforcers their behavior itself is the chief justification for their job. This is to say that it is not the rules that give meaning to their jobs, but rather the enforcement. As a consequence, built into the policeman's role is the inertia to behave as the enforcer, to bring about solutions by the imposition of force. In our society, this inertia can best find an outlet in the ghetto, in the community that is thought to be crime-ridden and therefore in need of the most serious enforcement of the law or the rules.

Certainly, police officers have a kind of crusading interest in stamping out evil, but it is probably much more typical for the officer to have a certain detached and objective view of his job. He is not likely to be concerned with the impact of any particular rule as he is with the fact that it is his job to enforce it. When the rules are changed, the officer punishes what was once acceptable behavior just as he ceases to punish behavior that has been made legitimate by a change in the rules. The basis for the officer's actions lies in the fact that the existence of the rule provides him with a job, a profession, and a raison d'etre.[2]

Recent changes in the drug law, like those for marijuana, and non-enforcement prescriptions of the laws for homosexual behavior and fornication indicates this point of how police can give up on a particular rule without a great deal of care or fuss. This is notwithstanding the fact that the deviant behavior of drug abuse is thought to be rampant in the ghetto. Policemen can, and do, have personal feelings about particular rules they are called upon to enforce, and this has ramifications in terms of the well-known problem of police discretion in the enforcement of laws. However, the fact that the policeman on the beat has the power of discretion in enforcing certain laws also attests to the importance that the policeman places upon being a rule enforcer. He sees himself as having the authority to validate or invalidate certain rules. That is the feeling of power, something that all rule enforcers must feel they have. The latitude for feelings of individual power and discretion in enforcing laws is at its widest in the ghetto. The ghetto, after all, is an outpost, the urban frontier where the asphalt cowboys are expected to roam.

It is the rules or the laws which give the police their justification for their jobs, their profession, their individual behaviors on the beat. This is contingent upon the fact that the enforcer has two interests which condition his enforcement activity. First, he must justify the existence of his position and, second, he must win the respect of those he deals with.

These attitudes are not peculiar to only rule enforcers. People of various occupations feel the need to justify their work and win the respect of others. Entertainment figures would like to do this, but they have difficulty in finding ways of successfully impressing their worth on the public who comes to see them. Even janitors want to win their tenants' respect, and they develop an ideology which stresses the quasi-professional responsibility they have to keep confidential the intimate knowledge of tenants they acquire in the course of their work. There are others like physicians, lawyers, and other professionals who are more successful in winning the respect of clients.

In trying to justify the reason and existence of his position in society, the rule enforcer is confronted with a double problem. He must, on the one hand, show that the problem which causes him to enforce the rules over those who break it, still exists. At the same time, he must also demonstrate that the problem he is supposed to be dealing with is being dealt with effectively. Therefore, you frequently find police organizations, especially at budget allocation times when they are seeking funds, jumping back and forth between the two claims. The police will say that they are making inroads in reducing crime, for instance, but in the same breath they find ways to say that the crime rate is rising, for reasons outside of their control, to be sure. Police officials will talk strongly about the good job their men are doing, but they are always ready to ask for more help and higher budgets because the problems that justify their existence are always ebbing from good to bad as a reason for the positions they occupy.

This attitude of the police, among other things, forces them to have a pessimistic view of human nature. It is easy to have such a view if you work in the ghetto. It is almost as though the police believe in original sin the way they can dwell on the difficulties in getting people to abide by the law, and their skepticism about attempts, in prisons and the like, to reform law-breakers. No group of people in our society seem to be more colored with original sin than the people of the ghetto. In the Western consciousness, at least going back to the medieval days of Europe, the color black has always had the symbolic reference of evil. Black stood for polluted evilness, and white stood for cleansing purity. It is the white cop who most frequently enters the black ghetto as a cleansing, protective agent for society.

The pessimistic outlook of the rule enforcer is reinforced by his daily experiences. From day to day, the purpose of his work is verified. The same people continually repeat offenses, thus definitely branding themselves in his eyes as outsiders. Nevertheless, it is not with too great a stretch of the imagination to suppose that one of the underlying reasons for the enforcer's pessimism about human nature and the possibilities of reform is the fact that if human nature were perfectible, his job would come to an end.

If the police feel compelled to look on the bad side of human nature, they also feel compelled to believe that it is necessary for the people they deal with to respect them. Without this respect, the police feel it would be difficult for them to do their job, and their feeling of security in their work will be totally lost. As a consequence, most of the enforcement activity is devoted not to the specific enforcement of rules, but rather to the coercing of respect from the people the enforcer deals with. As an outcome, this means that a person may be labeled as a deviant not because he has actually broken a rule, but because he has shown disrespect to the enforcer of the rule.

The policeman entering the ghetto sees himself as going into the enemy's camp. In order to do his job, and to do it well, a feeling of security and respect seems most necessary. A policeman whose beat is a white middle-class neighborhood does not have the same need. The sense of being threatened, walking into the enemy's camp, is not there. Therefore, there is less of a need, in fact a great deal less of a need, to sure up one's feelings of security while coercing the public into giving you respect.

Apart from the racial and subcultural attitudes police might have that can cause them to be more aggressive towards blacks and other minorities, it is likely in any event that they would act aggressively towards these groups to enhance their sense of security and gain the public display of respect from them that the police desire. Are the blacks, then, being supersensitive when they accuse the police of treating them differently, more harshly, than whites? Probably not. As rule enforcers, the police automatically find themselves juxtaposed to blacks and the ghetto. If they stop and frisk blacks more frequently than whites, for the most minimal of reasons, this is not harassment but rule enforcement. Minorities may complain about police brutality, but police say that their behavior is commensurate with the need to enforce the rules over those groups.

The rule enforcers in the ghetto are not members of that community. They are foreigners who come there to do a job. They are separated from the residents by the nature of their function, by the subculture that supports them, and by the social status that is generally attributed to those who fight to maintain the status quo. The rule enforcers in the ghetto, the police, that is, are generally despised by the residents, but more important they are suspiciously observed by the larger society. Social servants who work among the enemy in a community of institutionalized deviancy are likely, it is believed, to get the smell of the ghetto on them too. Can Serpico be wrong?[3] For this reason, there is the tendency for society at large to turn its back on the police who work in the ghetto. The police in the ghetto become a pariah group.[4]

SOCIAL BROKERS

The people of the ghetto are rejected people. The ghetto community is a social wastebasket. Nevertheless, the ghetto is an integral part of the American social scene. There is continuous interaction between the ghetto, its individual residents, and the larger society. The character of this interaction, the meeting of the bodies and the meeting of the minds is very much mediated by a corps of social brokers, of which the police are one group. Others are social workers, teachers, welfare caseworkers, parole and probation officers. Brokers are individuals who do not live in the ghetto but frequently visit it for the purpose of acting in some official capacity in order to promulgate the norms of the social mainstream.

Along with the promulgation of establishment norms, brokers also act as a buffer between the ghetto and the mainstream of society. Traditionally, people who have played this buffer role have also been referred to at various times as mediators, agents, middlemen, gatekeepers, fixers, facilitators (or inhibitors), and go-betweens. "They may be viewed at one extreme as facilitating the flow of information and even individuals between minority groups and the mainstream. At the other extreme they may be viewed as having a restrictive role in facilitating such flows and, in fact, as contributing to the isolation of particular minority groups from the mainstream."[5]

The police as a buffer, in terms of the ghetto, can readily be seen and understood when one recalls the events of the 1960s. During that period, it was generally believed that the ghetto was the cause of the rising crime rates and the social disturbances that were rocking the nation. The ghetto was the seat of the enemy camp. The strong arm of the police, the asphalt cowboys, were needed there. Without the police fighting it out with the urban guerrillas, where would those riots have taken us? Nevertheless, even though the police presence as a shock absorber in the 1960s is very well known, the full role of the police as a buffer is much more subtle, and to that degree much more effective.

For example, because the police stand as a symbol towards which the blacks in the ghetto can direct their free-floating animosity and enmity, relieving the pressures of their frustration, this is an act that helps to isolate the mainstream from the "crazy niggers." Because the police in the ghetto stand for the authority and power of existing institutions, their presence in that community with nightsticks and guns is in and of itself intimidating. This intimidation will likely put a certain amount of restraint on antiestablishment behavior of residents. This benefits the mainstream. The police are being used as a screen and precipitously deflecting black frustration.

In trying to define the causal elements of deviant behavior, social scientists have tended to take a very functional view of its origins. Deviance can only be understood in a social context, therefore, it must be a function of that context. The theories of Durkheim, Merton, Sutherland and Cressey, Reckless, and many others fall into this rather traditional way of describing the cause of deviancy, and indeed crime. Crime, of the pervasive, institutional kind, results, it is believed, primarily from low socioeconomic conditions in a given community. This idea is one of the chief motivating forces in the criminal justice system. Indeed, this is an attitude that is generally believed throughout our society. Knowing that the ghetto has the worst socioeconomic conditions in our society, it can be expected from this premise that crime and deviancy would be rampant there. From this point of view, the police in the ghetto have to be seen as a buffer by accident or design.

The role of the police as social broker can often be overlooked because their functions are not readily thought to be of welfare or social service practices. However, Police Athletic League (PAL) functions are seen nearer to this side, although the police function here is not, strictly speaking, official, but it is more a voluntary, off-duty responsibility that the individual policeman can choose to participate in. At the same time, those kids in the ghetto who participate in the PAL activities, like the Golden Gloves, are seen as the better kids by the policemen themselves, if for no other reason than the fact that the policemen who involve themselves in the activities come to know the boys. As a result, the police are ready to give good recommendations and maintain a lenient eye for boys they know. Quite a few young men have gone from the PAL ghetto clubs to boxing in the Olympics, and this has led to a few of them becoming well established later in the social mainstream. The youths turn professional boxers. They have a chance to become boxing champions. In these instances, the police were clearly the middlemen.

As a broker, here is another example of police influence in the ghetto. For a young person born in the ghetto, it is extremely important to stay out of trouble with the police. Trouble with the police can get you a police record, and that would be bad news. Why? Because the bridge from ghetto to social mainstream is there only for the youths who can grow up without any black marks against them, without any arrests. There are greater opportunities for success in education and jobs for the clean kid from the ghetto, and hardly any opportunities for "the bloods" who get police records. Given the fact that the police officer on the beat has a great deal of discretion in enforcing laws, certainly those related to youthful type offenses like criminal mischief, disorderly conduct, drinking under-age, and so on, they can be very influential in determining whether or not a young ghetto person gets a record or grows up clean. This is apart from whether or not the young person is given a sentence in a correctional institution. An arrest record has been known to follow a young person all of his life, even though he may not have been convicted of any specific offense.

Within these kinds of circumstances, the police are definitely acting as a broker. Those young people who do not grow up clean will likely spend the rest of their lives in a ghetto or prison, with few opportunities to break the vicious cycle once they obtain a police record.

But of course, the police brokering between minorities and the main-stream of society is not only a factor between the police and young people. Blacks who may have obtained positions of responsibility, whether they live in or out of the ghetto, young or old, may find their positions in jeopardy if they are arrested and/or accused of some crime. To lose that clean status means to suddenly be seen as an escapee from the ghetto. Former Representative Adam Clayton Powell from Harlem found this out in the late 1960s when the House leadership sought to get him for some of his outspoken stands on civil rights issues. Powell was toppled from power without much difficulty when he lost his clean status in Washington.

What we have already described as the role of the broker, and in this case, the policeman broker, can be seen in some very functional ways. In effect, the broker's role here is in part a task of recruiting from the ghetto for the mainstream. This recruiting is, of course, indirect. But, for example, the ghetto has long been a source of cheap labor. Those people of the ghetto who have had police contact, a record, are by and large not eligible for the better, higher paying jobs. Police records make people more likely to adopt some menial job that pays very little. It is these types of jobs that help to support the lifestyle of the white middle class. The types of jobs that people of the ghetto most readily take are jobs in the service industries: domestic work, restaurant work, hotel work, babysitting, nanny-type jobs. The beneficiaries of this is the white middle class.

Also, the people who have had police records and have been rebuffed in the job market because of it, in particular those individuals who have served time in prisons, are not likely to pursue jobs in the traditional markets for very long. After being rebuffed a number of times, these individuals may stop looking for "normal" ways to make a living. This means the traditional occupational system will not have to employ many blacks who need jobs because they will not even look for jobs they feel will be denied them. And even the U.S. Department of Labor will stop counting these individuals among the ranks of the unemployed because they stop looking for jobs.

Police activity in the ghetto, among other things, creates a pool of workers, and nonworkers who become eligible for legitimate or illegitimate employment. This results not so much from the enforcement of the laws, but rather the promulgation of social norms. It follows because policemen in the broker's role are *advocates* of mainstream values.

Indeed, the advocate role is tied very much into the role of recruiter. Think of it this way, those who are recruited into the mainstream are not likely to have police records, and the way you avoid having a police record is by adhering to the police concept of mainstream values. Because policemen are mostly lower-middle class whites, they tend to hold very strongly to mainstream values like the work ethic, religious faith, monogamy, heterosexuality, and so on. The police, in attitude, demeanor, and in enforcement of the laws, exhibit mainstream social preferences. The ghetto offers itself as a unique opportunity for the police to promulgate social values.

Advocating the social preferences of the mainstream may be just as important, if not more so, to police work as so-called crime fighting. From one point of view it is definitely more important than crime fighting. The policeman's advocation of these preferences becomes a hallmark, a measurement for ghetto youngsters to compare themselves with. In this way, the police brokers are acting as agents for cultural transmission. This broker attribute is very much exampled in the PAL activities of the police. In PAL the police officer's participation is held up as an example for youths to follow. In this role policemen are overtly trying to transmit the values and traditional behaviors of the mainstream.

Police as brokers often become advocates for the rights and needs of the ghetto minority. PAL is a way in which this is done. Other ways this can come about is through police sponsored boys' clubs, fresh air funds for city-bound kids, and police officers playing "Big Brother" to fatherless youths. In these roles, the policemen as brokers appear as benevolent forces in the ghetto community, a role that invites admiration and respect from residents. But at the same time, the fundamental role of the police, as agents of society in a community that is thought to contain institutionalized deviancy, is never eclipsed. A policeman who is a PAL instructor can be the same person who will arrest violators of the law. In this capacity, the police are playing the roles of both friend and foe.

THE URBAN COLONIAL GUARD

Kenneth B. Clark in his book *Dark Ghetto* described the black ghetto as a colony. The dark ghettos are social, political, educational, and economic colonies. In such a context, the police are agents of colonial rule, placed in the ghetto to ensure societal control of the community. Continuing along this type of social axis, the police must then inevitably work against black attempts to free themselves from colonial rule. Black attempts to decolonize their social existence was strongly resisted by the police in the 1960s. Civil rights demonstrators, particularly in the South, came to be seen as a special kind of law breaker. They were worse than felons. They were un-American, and therefore they deserved to be squashed like bedbugs. The point is clear. Blacks had to break the law to bring about social change for their own betterment.

The colonial guard status of the police calls upon them to inhibit "the native community" from social, political, and economic coalescences. The rationalizations the police might use for doing this are many. It might be based on the subculture status of the police, their law and order mandate, and/or the myth of socially controlling a communicable disease. But, then again, colonial guards do not need any other reasons for their behavior except that of the ongoing community's threat of decolonization of the ghetto, which is a natural outgrowth of the fact that ghetto residents are kept out of the social mainstream.

Ghetto residents are not, strictly speaking, inculcators of the values of the mainstream because it is those values which symbolize their repression. The police, as colonial guards, are responsible for pulling the ghetto residents back to the center of society, by force if necessary, so that they might be bathed in the acceptable, traditional values.[6] In making an arrest for nonmajor felonies, the policeman does so probably as much from a sense of rejected values as he does because he feels he must uphold the law. The policeman attempts to reinforce the values of the social mainstream by punishing those who do not adhere to those values.

Colonization is an act of forcing new values on an indigenous population by an outside, alien cultural force. Decolonization is therefore a rejection of those values. Decolonization is the meeting of two powerful social forces, opposed to each other by their very natures. So, attempts by blacks to create a new set of values which would remove them from a colonized consciousness is to be resisted by society at large, and the police in particular.

Societal and police resistance to black decolonization can be seen in the case of the Black Muslims. The Muslims' ideology states that it is the major task of the Nation of Islam to awaken the American black man to his destiny. He must be alerted to false prophets, especially those who call for integration. Integration is but a plot of the white people to prevent their own doom. The black bourgeoisie, having been bought off by a few paltry favors and attempting to ingratiate themselves to the whites, seek to spread this pernicious doctrine among the so-called Negroes. The Nation believed that it had to encourage blacks to begin now to assume their proper role by wresting economic control from the whites.

Blacks had to gain control over their own economic fortunes by going into business for themselves and becoming economically strong. The Nation of Islam had to encourage the so-called Negroes to give up those habits which had been spread among them by the whites as part of the effort to keep them weak, diseased, and demoralized. Blacks had to give up such white-fostered, dissolute habits as drinking, smoking, and eating improper foods, and they had to seek a land of their own within the continental United States. The Nation believed that this land was due them and would free blacks from the pernicious influences of the whites.

The statement from the Nation of Islam uses black-white descriptions, but the ideology essentially follows the mandate that was laid down in the Declaration of Independence in 1776.

When in the course of human events it becomes necessary for one people to dissolve the political bonds which have connected them with another, and to assume among the powers of the earth, the separate and equal station to which the Laws of Nature and of Nature's God entitle them, a decent respect to the opinions of mankind requires that they should declare the causes which impel them to the separation.

However, the Declaration is a mandate for decolonization.

The Kerner Commission, in search of causes and culprits of the 1960s urban riots, took a look at the Black Muslims and commented: One of the major factors intensifying the Civil Rights Movement was widespread black unemployment and poverty; an important force in awakening black protest was the meteoric rise to national prominence of the Black Muslims, established around 1930. The Black Muslims reached the peak of their influence when more progress toward equal rights was being made than ever before in American history while at the same time economic opportunity for the poorest groups in the urban ghettos was stagnating.

The commission continued: Increasing unemployment among blacks, combined with the revolution in expectations, created a climate in which the Black Muslims thrived. They preached a vision of doom of the white devils and the coming dominance of the black man. They promised a utopian paradise of a separate territory within the United States for black people, and offered a practical program of building black business through hard work, thrift, and racial unity. For those people who were willing to submit to the rigid discipline of the movement, the Black Muslim organization gave a sense of purpose and dignity.

The commission's overall evaluation of the Black Muslims has to be seen as negative. In fact, the writer seems to be smirking behind his hand when he speaks of the Muslims preaching the doom of the white devils, the coming dominance of the black man, and a separate state for blacks in America. "Hah, ha . . . can you believe that bull . . . .!"

Declaration of Independence or no, to the police the Black Muslims were another one of those un-American groups that had to be treated like a rattlesnake. Of course, if you want to believe it, the police attitude had nothing to do with the fact that the ideology of the Muslims was a program for decolonization. Rattlesnakes are hated for being rattlesnakes. They are not hated for wanting to be free rattlesnakes, and like the rattlesnakes, the Muslims could become lethal if they were not watched and controlled very carefully. Do you remember what happened to Malcolm X? And if that is not enough, the adverse publicity from the slaying of Malcolm X still supports the erroneous notion that the Muslims preach violence.

In the colonial world of the ghetto, there are always frontiers, separation points between the ghetto community and the rest of society. Harlem has its 110th Street (although the ghetto has crept beyond it now), and Philadelphia had its South Street and Columbia Avenue, the former having resisted the ghetto tide and the latter having succumbed to it. Every large city in America has its frontiers of separation, and the police tend to be commonplace and frequent on such streets, or near to them. The colonial world has always been divided into two, and along the dividing line one always found the police or the army. Sometimes a park, train tracks, or river would be the dividing line, and the police would not have to be so numerous right at the point of separation. And frequently, the border area would be a shopping commercial district, like Columbia Avenue and South Street were, which meant that the police were always there in goodly numbers to protect the commercial establishments, and *inadvertently* to protect the frontiers.

Perhaps, in big cities today, more than streets being the dividing lines between the ghetto and the nonghetto areas, what you really find is that the divisions are constituted by transportation links—subways, buses, and trolley lines. Those lines that go directly into the ghetto are usually heavily patrolled by the police. When entering or exiting the ghetto by one of these links, it is likely that one will see a policeman.

The fact that the urban ghetto is considered to be a violent community may well be as much a sign of the existence of the community's colonial status as it is seemingly recognized as a place of institutionalized deviancy. Violence has always been prevalent in colonized communities. It is the policeman or the soldier who is the official sanctioned go-between, the spokesman of the overclasses to the underclasses.[7] This spokesmanship is made evident and realizable by the ever-present potential of violent supervision. The policeman in combat dress, the club, the gun, the handcuffs.

Colonizers must set a tone in their supervisions, a tone that displays a willingness to use force. In the ghetto, without provocation, at some time or another the police must display force or their potential to do so will not be recognized. It is a commonly known fact that the people of the ghetto think that the police act too much in cavalier fashion in their neighborhoods. At the same time, the police admit that they believe the minority community needs greater supervision because deviancy is much more flagrant in the ghetto community. The question is whether or not the police as colonial guards function in a manner that, of necessity, must precipitate the use of force, separate and apart from any specific criminal action that may require their attention.

Some of the society's common attitudes toward the police bespeaks of their colonial guard responsibilities. For example, traditionally the frontline forces of colonialistic imperialism, the colonial guards, were expendable. They were men and women, in terms of the missionary ladies who forged into Africa and the Orient, making way for European enterprises that were to follow, who were sent far from their native shores to do service for their government. They went to the outposts, the frontiers, the social wilderness. They were usually loudly heralded but minimally rewarded. They were persons of high political regard, but of little social status.

Today our society tends to look at its colonial guards in the same way. We make a big fuss about them—they are New York's finest. They usually have bad working conditions, low pay relative to responsibilities, and mortal endangerment is part of their daily jobs. They are frequently expected to function far from the mainstream of society, and it is not unusual for a policeman to work out his full career on society's frontier, the urban frontier, the urban ghetto.

As violence was expected to be a part of the colonial world—King Leopold II of the Belgians knew this—colonial guards by their nature were expendable. Being a guard, one's reason for allowing oneself to be expendable lay in the appeal of God and country, the fatherland, the maintenance of civilization, the preservation of the white race, law and order. But today, the reason most often given is the desire for financial security, a steady paycheck, and even worse, a retirement check. The chauvinist ideal, a sense of nationalism, is not the critical measure in the rationalizations of the police who must work in the ghetto. The police like to think of themselves as working for a wage first, and society second. Have our urban colonial guards become a pack of selfish mercenaries?

STRATIPHILES

Policemen have an extraordinary concern for the social ranks of the specific publics being served. Status, class, and caste are active modalities in police work. It begins with the fact that they see people in good-bad terms, the perpetrator and the victim, and it begins with the fact that the police are always looking for clues which will help them determine who is the good guy and who is the bad guy. Apart from the policeman's work, our society of course has its ranking system, or stratification system, which is based on money, education, profession, race, religion, ethnicity, and certainly color. "If you're white, you're alright. If you're brown, stick around. If you're black get back."

Policemen are also acutely aware of social ranks because police power is essentially a manipulated, political tool. Further, the strength of politics is based on vested interest, and vested interest owes its allegiance to power that comes from social rank. Vested interest is also guardian of the status quo. Higher rankings are given to individuals who protect the system. This means that policemen will tend to be a force for conservatism rather than liberalism. In a society that professes democratic ideals, directions along the political spectrum are also factors in the social ranking process.

Personally, policemen tend to have a strong attachment to rank identities. As symbols for the common good, for law and order, they have a recognizable status that means a great deal to them. Their attachment to this recognized status probably flows from the fact that policemen tend to come to the police force with a strong belief in the existence of a higher authority in the best Calvinist tradition. Max Weber has pointed out that this belief forms one of the roots of our hierarchical system of authority. The policeman accepts the right of certain individuals to have authority over him, his commanders, the chief or commissioner of the department, and perhaps the mayor. But at the same time, he maintains the right to have authority over others, the civilians, the assholes, who are animals at worst and at best do not have his capacity for quick decisions and effective action.

To the policeman, the world is a stratified world, the society is a stratified society, and the community is a stratified community. Only stratified authority can maintain law and order. This is a dedicated view of the world, a view that can take precedence over all others. Social stratification has intimate meaning to police officers because it is a view of the world on which they may have to stake their lives. In doing their work, the dependency of the police upon social stratification bears out this fact. In every sense of the word, policemen are *stratiphiles;* that is, individuals who are extraordinarily disposed to the forces and commitments that flow from social stratification. This disposition has very definite consequences for the black ghetto.

Social scientists generally believe that societies rank their members because they are confronted with limited resources. A given social system wants to determine who, and with what qualifications, has lesser or greater access to these resources. The resources one referred to are those basic resources needed by all to ensure physical, psychological, and emotional survival. In America that means income, and for most Americans, that means the quality of his or her job. Because individuals without police records are seen as more employable than those with police records in our society, and because policemen tend to have a great deal of discretion in initiating the arrest procedure, particularly in the ghetto, the police then are brokers between citizens, and the means of their survival. Blacks have long been aware of this, and it is one of the reasons they can feel so antagonistic towards the police in respect to the police abusing their prerogatives in black communities.

The police, and indeed the entire criminal justice system, tends to treat poor people much more harshly than affluent ones. Recognition of social ranking is certainly at work here, and it is consistent with the operations of stratified systems that demand some groups be favored over others. Being given special favors is one aspect of an affluent lifestyle. Conversely, nonaffluent lifestyles are easily recognized because there tends to be the absence of favoritism in the lifestyle. Clearly the police are exercising a type of power, discretionary power, in their unequal treatment of citizens. This is to say that stratification provides the basis for certain types of power, the power of one group to be treated better than another, the power of one group to directly dominate another.

Policemen can have a great deal of discretion in their work in the ghetto because ghetto residents are ranked at the very bottom of the social scale. Ghetto residents are considered to be social throwaways, say some observers, so as long as they can be kept out of sight, they will remain out of mind. This fact also addresses itself to the lack of power among ghetto residents, a lack of power in almost any socially meaningful term.

One of the ways to look at the differential qualities of power from one group to another is to see it in terms of class. Max Weber's definition of class is the one to be used here. Weber used the idea of class to mean specifically a group's economic or lack of economic power. Can the group work its will in the marketplace? No, the people in the ghetto cannot work their will in the marketplace, and the police know this. The police think of ghetto residents as made up of people who are largely on the dole, on welfare, or involved in some other kind of hustle.[8] They have no economic power because most of the jungle bunnies cannot hold down a job. Even the small businesses in the ghetto are more often than not owned by outside white interests. Further, it is well known that the highest rates of unemployment are to be found in the ghetto. You cannot have economic power unless you have a job. Blacks are likely to have fewer jobs than other social groups, and when they do have jobs, the jobs will tend to be menial, lowpaying service type employment. There is no economic power here that is likely to be respected by police authorities.

As stratiphiles, the police would be very conscious of anything that tended to distinguish the rich from the poor. This is why they are very cognizant of any individual or group's status or lack thereof. Weber says that the status of any group comes from their social power or their ability to demand respect and preferential treatment from others. By being black and of the ghetto, the only thing that the resident is likely to command from other social groups is either disrespect or sympathy. The only preferential treatment the ghetto resident is likely to get is that which will probably serve him negatively—like police brutality, de facto segregation, lack of job opportunities, educational opportunities, and other ongoing discriminations. The police are not likely to have anything but negative feelings about a group who has as little status in society as ghetto blacks. Their stratiphilic attitude will demand it of them.

There is another strong means by which power can be indicated in our society, a means that the police are sure to respect. This is power that comes from the party, says Weber, or the political groups or constituency.[9] Political power comes from the group's ability to work their wills through the various organs of government.[10] Under these terms, surely the police are not going to give anything more than superficial recognition to the black power of the ghetto. It tends to represent form more than substance as the true mechanisms of community control and decision making tend to remain downtown in the mayor's office, or at the state capitol, or in Washington, D.C. The police are very familiar with this, as are most

Americans. There are still, relative to their overall population numbers, very few blacks in significant political offices. For all practical purposes, the blacks have little or no direct political power of their own. And, if, and when, the blacks get too much out of line, as was the case with the riots of the sixties, the emergence of the Black Panthers and the Black Muslims as national forces, black political power will be totally ignored by the establishment, whatever its substance or character. When blacks become a threat to the white establishment, they have no political power, which is normally the case for social groups at the bottom of the ranking system. This is why they become objects of freely expressed scorn. They are expected to be looked down on and treated differently. The police do no more than follow the dictates of the stratification system.

An example of how the police are dictated to by the ranking system can be seen in the following way. The police, as we have said, have a great deal of discretion in how they might deal with offenders or suspected offenders of the law. Whites in general, and the police most certainly, harbor certain unfavorable stereotypes about ghetto residents. The stereotypes are especially an outgrowth of our society's stratification system. The lower in rank, the more nasty and bigoted will be the description in the stereotype. After all, police think of blacks as coons, head hunters, jungle bunnies, and mau mau. This causes the police to look at black behavior, particularly in the ghetto, in an expecting, accepting way, even when the behavior results in the breaking of laws. "You know, that is the way the blacks are."

Legal discrimination that is based on such stereotypes can produce a deprivation of civil rights of a more subtle nature as well. White stereotypes of minority group members as being "just that way" in relation to criminal behavior may lead to a condoning of acts of violence or petty theft. Since the victims of such acts are likely to be members of the same ethnic group, minority people may find themselves without sufficient police and court protection against being victimized by fellow ethnics.

In a traditional, Southern white community, the white stereotype of black sexual mores stresses the sexual promiscuity of blacks, especially black women. Therefore, it is difficult to convince a white judge and jury to believe that a black woman could be raped. It is assumed that the woman is always willing to be "victimized" by any and all comers. Similarly, women say it is difficult to prosecute a rapist because of the suspicion of the victim's own involvement and willingness. The "blacks will be blacks" attitude of police officers works both against this group in terms of getting proper protection and in making them perpetrators most likely for prosecution.

Most policemen start out their careers with a great deal of respect for the position they are about to assume and the role they think they will play in society. Then the rude reality awakens them. They may find themselves in a ghetto where social etiquette dictates disrespect of the policeman. This social situation will call upon the cop to protect his personal dignity, to save face, and the way this is done is by getting the ghetto residents to show him respect. It is a natural expectation of the police officer because of his higher position in society. Stratification demands that the police officer be shown certain respect while, you might say, the ghetto residents be shown a kind of equal proportion of disrespect. A person has a right to protect his "honor." For the policeman on the beat in the ghetto, this can mean getting the resident to honor his authority. For a ghetto resident who may view the police as pigs and who is openly hostile to and alienated from the authority structures and legal norms of society, resisting police authority may be one of the most honorable acts he may feel he can socially commit. From their different perspectives each is trying to force certain compliance from the other to protect his honor. Because of the stratification system in society, however, and the legality of the police officer's public position, the weight of the exchange is decidedly on the side of the policeman.

This type of relationship, policeman to ghetto resident, that favors the policeman, is a type of discriminatory etiquette that was described by Erving Goffman in his book *Asylums*. In total institutions, the higher honor attributed to staff persons is symbolized in echelon terms of authority, or *any* staff member over *any* patient. In the same way, *any* police officer has the right to exercise authority over *any* citizen. The importance of this fact takes shape here when this activity is seen in terms of classes or whole groups of people. If higher ranked individuals believe they have the right to be shown respect by lower ranked individuals, in this case the police officer by the ghetto resident, the psychological deprivation of belonging to a category of lesser social honor becomes obvious. It is the police officer who can make the resident feel uncomfortable by expressing his authority in such a way as to elicit the respect he desires from the ghetto individual.

It is axiomatic that blacks have experienced such assaults on their dignity by the police. Take the matter of the way the police will address blacks as an illustration. Police will frequently address black men as "boy" rather than "mister" or "sir." Any police officer can thus speak to any black male that way, but the black male is expected to address the policeman as "officer" or "sir," any policeman. The generic root of boy goes back to the strong segregation days of the South. Blacks had to be shown their place when with a white. Comparably, black women were called girls. Of course, the situation becomes rather awkward when a police officer confronts a black who is clearly of higher social status than himself, a fact that would be immediately recognized if the person were white. The police officer can get around this situation by exaggerating the status of the black person all out of proportion. The black person may be called "doctor" or "professor" or "prez." This minimizes the real status.

Social stratification can dictate behavior and dictate responses. It sets the character and tone of relationships through the uses of stereotypes. In some of our social relations, it makes mechanical men out of us all. For the policeman in the ghetto, there are many pressures on him to do his work in accordance with this society's system of stratification, and much evidence would indicate that to a large measure the policeman does just that.

MARGINAL MEN

A body of literature in race and ethnic studies addresses itself to the concept of the "marginal man." The concept is used to refer to one of the social dilemmas of minority group members, living in a dominant culture, but also being a member of a subculture. The minority person has grown up with the aspirations and goals of the dominant culture, but at the same time he is being blocked from full participation in the society and the attainment of those goals. The marginal man is one who is hemmed in on two sides by two cultures, each of which is putting pressure on him to conform to its social edicts and norms to the denial of the other. The psychological difficulties for the marginal man are further exacerbated by the fact that he is estranged from a firm sense of social identity because at least two sets of cultural values are making demands on him.

While the idea of the marginal man is usually applied to minority group members, social scientists also recognize that the consequences of marginality are not limited to minority group members. Our society is rapidly changing from year to year. There is a lack of a stable, continuous, unchallenged set of life definitions that makes virtually everyone, to a lesser or greater degree, a marginal person.[11] Accepting this basic comment, a special case of marginality, I believe, can be made for policemen, and it has special relationship to their working in the black ghettos.

The policemen are certainly persons who find themselves a part of the dominant culture but at the same time they are members of a subculture. Indeed, they are members of the police subculture, but if they work in the ghetto and they learn the ways of ghetto life as they must, there will be pressures on them to conform to this subculture as well. Not only are policemen fully inculcated with the aspirations of the dominant culture, but they are also called upon to guard and protect the values upon which those aspirations sit. Working in the ghetto, the policeman can easily conclude that the community constitutes a threat to society's cherished values. Because of this, the policeman may feel compelled to "throw his weight around," to let people know that he may walk the same streets with them, but he is something different, something better.

The policeman may want to keep himself emotionally and psychologically separated from the culture of the ghetto, but the task may be totally impossible. Within the being and mind of the ghetto cop, two cultures, if not three, overlap. The officer in this manner must partake of them all. When he is responding to a situation, he will call upon his smarts, if need be, without cultural distinction. For example, the policeman in the ghetto is likely to have come from a working-class background that socialized him to seek physical rather than verbal solutions to conflicts. At the same time, the police subculture of the officer has taught him how to use force to resolve conflicts. Add to this fact that aggression, police to residents, and residents to police, tends to be an active modality in the ghetto, and you have the power of overlapping cultural forces. If the policeman has to take physical action against a perpetrator, he will be calling upon the fruition of all these forces.

This is not to suggest that harmony exists for the marginal man when his two or more cultures overlap. In fact, there is more likely to be conflict between them. The policeman in the ghetto finds himself adopting the mannerisms and language of that community over time. It is a necessity of his work. He must be able to communicate with the people very quickly in trying to control situations, protect residents, and be supportive of them. But those same mannerisms must be altered when that policeman is in his middle-class neighborhood, off the job. However, the policeman cannot easily disengage himself from his street mannerisms, and as Arthur Niederhoffer puts it, the role comes to dominate his life. As the policeman attempts to be an active member of different cultures, he must of necessity cause an intermingling of the different cultural values. This can cause him certain psychological and emotional trauma. The feelings of a marginal individual are likely to be that of insecurity, ambivalence, excessive self-consciousness, and chronic nervous strain.

It is interesting to note that the feelings just described of a marginal person are feelings that are conventionally attributed to the policeman. We do not have to play with the chicken and egg question to understand that marginality is supported by conventional police attributes and conventional police attributes support marginality.

Continuing this line of thinking, marginality is thought to be a result of the conditioning of a person existing on the border of two cultures. For the policeman, the idea of living and participating in two cultures is constantly reinforced by the attitude the cop has of being a good guy in a bad guy's world. The ghetto sharpens this entire focus for the police officer. The ethnicity of the people, their habits, their lifestyle, their color, all tell the policeman that the culture of his job community is something different than the culture and community he calls his own. The residents of the ghetto community are not going to be applauded by the police for encouraging feelings of marginality. In fact, the contrary is likely to be the case.

Of course, marginality is also a description of a type of relating that can exist between individuals and groups. Marginal relationships address themselves to shallow, uncaring, superficial, impersonal types of human relating. Such characteristics can be easily used to describe the relations of police to the ghettos. Since the police may be seen as oppressors and pigs, there is little incentive for them to be anything more than marginal workers in the ghetto community. But this marginality is a bone of contention for the residents of the ghetto. The residents believe that individuals who are marginal in their relations to the ghetto, like the police, are not going to care about the community. "There can be no dialogue with strangers," some community leaders have said.

The marginality of the police to the black community can be seen in terms of the following kinds of facts. In New York City, traditionally none of the police officers who worked out of a ghetto precinct lived in that jurisdiction. The policemen of New York City tended to live in the outlying bedroom communities of Nassau and Suffolk counties. Only a few black officers might live in adjacent communities to the ghetto neighborhoods where they worked.

When a policeman's work day is over, the tour of duty ended, he will precipitously leave the neighborhood. Indeed, his exit can be so rapid it appears as though he is escaping from incarceration. There is usually no fraternization, no social mixing between the police and residents. They show no real interest in community problems. While the officers will talk about the bad conditions of their work community, littered streets, the incidence of violence and drug addiction, their concern is usually passive. When the job ends, the bad conditions are no longer their problems even to discuss. It is the residents who have to help themselves.

In general, the police think very little of community relations, particularly if it means keeping them in the ghetto neighborhood after their tour of duty has ended.

An event which had occurred in the beginning of 1966 exemplifies the temper of the men towards the idea of community relations. A former precinct captain, attempting to bridge the police/community gulf, arranged for a religious function at which community leaders would be honored. Only 20 of the 250 members of the precinct (including his personal and clerical staff) made an appearance. The reason (as reported subsequently) . . . was the felt hypocrisy of trying to use a religious ceremony to promote understanding and interest.[12]

The following is a further comment on the feelings of marginality that policemen can have in working in the ghetto. The comment was made by a former policeman who worked in Spanish Harlem in New York City during the activist period of the 1960s. It was customary, he said, to characterize ghetto residents as alienated from the mainstream of society. However, the ghetto child comes home from the strange, cold school environment to familiar streets, the security of his neighborhood, friends, and family. On the other hand, it is the police officer who is not of ghetto origin, and he feels a strong sense of nonbelonging and his negative attitudes towards residents are an outgrowth of this. Yes, in the poverty areas of East Harlem there were residents with feelings of isolation from the larger society, but that society was not their own. What alienated the residents was more the fact that they were being supervised by representatives of that larger society, the police and others. But what alienated the police was the supervising of alienated people.

Marginality, along with the other social forces discussed in this chapter, explains how the cop in the ghetto comes to his beat very much predisposed to perform in certain ways. To feel lonely and scared, to feel cut off from one's cultural roots in what is believed to be a hostile environment can deeply affect behavior. A police officer in the ghetto does not walk around on his beat, or ride in a patrol car, with the concepts we have discussed at the upper levels of his consciousness. Indeed, that is what gives more impetus to our story. For not only is this an attempt to acquaint nonpolice personnel with the intimacy of police behavior in the ghetto, but it is hoped that this treatise can enlighten the policemen themselves about attitudes that are largely taken for granted, and perhaps largely misunderstood.

CHAPTER 4

POLICE ROLES

WHITE ACTORS

The politicians and decision makers of our society would prefer not to think about the problems of the ghetto. They ignore the fact that the problems of the ghetto are but a reflection of the problems of America as a whole. Nothing of any long-range, meaningful consequence can be done about the ghetto until some very fundamental changes are made in American society. But until that happens, if it ever does, the ghetto must be maintained as an institutional scrapheap where society can junk its human throwaways. As a social institution, the ghetto has its attendants. We spoke of them, the social brokers, in the last chapter. Chief among this attendant corps are the police. It is the police who make possible much of the work of the other social brokers.

In this sense, the police are a connecting rod for the other social brokers, and to this degree they are servicing many different social functions. The larger police role in the ghetto is therefore made up of many sub-roles. One can study the work of the police in the black community from the larger or sub-role perspectives, and throughout this chapter we will be looking at police work from both these angles.

The police are a tremendous social force in the ghetto. Because of the role they play, they are social lynchpins. However, the role of social lynchpin is by its nature difficult and ambivalent. For instance, there is a definite element of self-sacrifice and expendability connected to the role that tends to diminish the actor. The following statement addresses itself to the diminishing character of the role. "It is not what I am that is important, but what is important is what I do." Thus speaks the policeman, the rule enforcer. This is the essence, the vitality, for better or worse, of police work in the ghetto.

PARIAHS

Policemen come to the ghetto as rule enforcers. They do not come to be nice, friendly, or neighborly. They come to do a job, as professionals, and to that degree they are like mercenaries. The policemen in the ghetto see themselves as working in an alien community. The residents of the ghetto see the policemen as aliens working in their community. In this context, the police are disassociated from the community, the people, and their culture. This status is further confirmed because the people of the community reject the police. Consequently, policemen who work in the ghetto do so as "pariah people," [1] and this is a unique social situation in our society.

However, the policemen are not only pariah people in respect to the ghetto community. They are seen as a pariah people in terms of the larger society. People who live, work in, or revere a marginal social system often become objects of suspicion and therefore are seen as different, as misfits, outcasts, and people separated from the mainstream.

The pariah character of the police bears a distinct social image for the ghetto residents. The police come to the ghetto with authority and legitimation, but at the same time they come as individuals who have no autonomous power of their own. Yes, they can use their clubs, guns, and make arrests, and that is an expression of power, but at the same time they are civil servants, men and women in blue, who are but acting out the mandate of their department, or carrying out the policies of their political overseers of the moment, i.e., the asphalt cowboys of the 1960s being instructed to ride the urban range of crime and disorder.

For the oppression that ghetto residents may feel, the police are to be blamed for the part they play, but at the same time they can be seen as blameless. This attitude can be found in a statement made by James Baldwin, when he said, "It is hard, on the other hand, to blame the policeman, blank, good-natured, thoughtless, and insuperably innocent, for being such a perfect representative of the people he serves." [2]

As the ghetto residents may direct their free-floating aggression towards policemen, at the same time the policemen themselves can appear as free-floating social entities in the social sea, free-floating like flotsam and jetsam. They come to the ghetto not as individuals who are acting out, specifically, the edicts of their own judgment and own will. Of course, the individual judgment and will is there because we are talking about human beings. However, too much of the person's judgments become the support system for an identity that comes with the uniform in blue.

It is the uniform the residents relate to, not the person who is inside it.

In the same way, the police officer, on duty in the ghetto, or perhaps this is true of a cop wherever his duty station might be, does not relate to himself as *wearing a uniform,* but instead he relates to himself as *being in uniform.* The term being connotes existence, and that is exactly what is intended by the phrase. When the uniform is worn, a certain kind of person comes into existence, a person who is a very special social entity. The pariah status is but one characteristic of it, a characteristic that allows the person to be imbued with a mystique that supports the special social function.

For the policeman, being a pariah is a function of the uniform. Pariah people are in society, but at the same time they are outside of it. Their behavior is not expected to conform to the general norms. Special allowances are to be made for pariah people. They can be secretive and bizarre, and still not raise social ire if it is kept among the group. The Jews were seen this way in feudal Europe, and as the outcast group they were locked up in ghettos. Policemen are seen in this way today, and this image is enhanced if they work in the ghetto; i.e., Serpico.

Pariah people as a group are cut off from the societal mainstream. Because of this, their association with people like themselves becomes a matter of fighting off social isolation. Being in uniform for the police officer is a statement of camaraderie between himself and the other boys in blue. The uniform symbolizes the raison d'etre that holds the police associations and comradeship together. The uniform can take on a sacred quality. Any questioning of the purposes of that uniform are likely to be met with a "punching out," or agressive–defensive behavior like that of frisking without probable cause and demanding that residents submit to police authority, as Paul Chevigny put it. The police purposes in the ghetto are questioned automatically by the residents. This causes the police to cling to their pariah status, and at the same time it causes them to punch out at the residents.

The social psychology of the pariah is dichotomous and ambivalent. On the one hand, the pariah feels looked down on and disrespected, but on the other hand, he feels superior to those who would see him in a lower social status than his own. Indeed, the pariah will tend to see his role in society with a great sense of mission and purpose, frequently associating this mission with divine intent—like preventing anarchy and saving Western civilization from lawlessness. We should not forget that our civilization was given credence by the son of God himself when he gave Westerners Christianity.

This type of vocational zeal, very much an outgrowth of the Protestant ethic, is very much an expression of one's *calling.* [3] Policemen speak of themselves as the last bastion of morality in a decadent society or the thin blue line holding back the seas of anarchy. Policemen like to say that all their lives they wanted to do some kind of work that would allow them to help people. Being a cop was the way to help people.

But this philosophy is confronted in the ghetto with a wave of protest, silent as a stare in many cases, but protest nevertheless. The police do help the residents, but they are also the rule enforcers who maintain society's control over the ghetto. That is to say, residents question the social legitimacy of the policeman's calling. This may be perceived by the policeman as a personal attack upon him by those who would question his calling. Such questioning inevitably impinges upon the officer's emotional commitment to his work.

To call a policeman a pig was to identify him as an establishment minion, one who came to the ghetto not because of his calling, but rather because the social forces that dominate society assigned him to that community. To be called a pig is scurrilous enough, but to be called a pig as a means of separating the cop from his sense of calling, his duty, can be a nullifying blow to his ego and self-presence. The response of the ghetto cop is to show an unflinching disgust for the public being served. The nerve of ghetto people questioning the calling of the police, they who have the lowest status in society. Our Protestant value system tells us that ghetto people have no calling. Their failure in life indicates this, along with the fact that they are less godly than other groups in society, and certainly less godly than police. Actually, this is another form of labeling; or if you will, the rattlesnake syndrome once again, but for the pariah mentality this is just acknowledging a fact of nature.

Pariah people tend to exhibit a general jealousy for people not of the group they associate with. These nonpariah people are recognized members of society. The pariah people are not. Jealousy is an evocation of stress between individuals and groups in society. There is a natural element of stress between the pariah status of the police officer and civilians, but this is very particular to the ghetto. Police officers tend to be envious of civilians who live normal lives and are accepted as being normal people. Even the ghetto is normal as a community where black people live in large numbers. It has its place in the total structure of society. The police are the outcast group in the ghetto, and they do not appreciate it.

The jealousy, as pariahs, that the police can feel towards ghetto residents can be identified in a statement made earlier in this book by a cop who worked in a ghetto. "It is customary to characterize ghetto residents as alienated from the mainstream of our culture. But the ghetto child comes home from the strange cold school atmosphere to the reality, familiarity, and security of his street, his friends, and his family. On the other hand, the policeman who is not of ghetto origin feels a strong sense of nonbelonging and his negative attitudes are outgrowths of this."

History tells us that a pariah people were a vengeful people, and like the Jews they often made appeals to God to bring down His wrath and punish the heathens, the nonbelievers. Pariah people have a need for vengeance because they have a need to punish. They come to feel that they cannot gain respect, their place in the community, unless punishment is meted out to the nonbelievers. In this case the nonbelievers are the ghetto residents, those who live by tarnishing the law, and who deny the policeman's calling.

Like the pariahs who appealed to their God, the police appeal to their higher authority, their commanders, their chief or commissioner, the mayor, and the public, for punishment of the nonbelievers—because vengeance must be theirs. This is not a call for the punishment of law breakers as such, that is a general call, but it is a particular call to punish those who draw attention to the policeman's pariah status. Therefore, the ghetto takes on the quality of being a haven for nonbelievers and heretics in a religious sense. It is a community that is infested with the disease of antisocial behavior. It becomes a symbol of lawlessness. With this type of labeling to legitimate their behavior, the pariah people, the policemen, can reap their vengeance.

Remember, the pariah status is a hurt and a pain, and the pariah people are deeply motivated to return that hurt and that pain. And this is yet another reason why policemen feel very comfortable with the notion that blacks and other ethnic minorities need more, and stronger, supervision than whites and some other social groups. You have to lean hard on jungle bunnies to make them heel. They have a built in proclivity to bite the hand that feeds them.

For pariah people, their vocation or job is their only real source of security. Since the job of the policeman is a calling, success in the job is a matter of proof of the dignity and legitimacy of that calling. The ghetto environment produces the greatest sense of pariah status for the police, and as a consequence the police will try harder to be successful in this community because there will be a greater sense of emotional need to show proof of the dignity and legitimacy of their calling. The ghetto being filled with jungle bunnies is just ripe to fulfill this proof.

Pariah people will tend to have an abiding respect for wealth and money. Wealth is a meaningful way for them to establish a self-presence, a place in society. Witness the Jews in history establishing themselves in banking. It is only natural to be drawn to the social factors and means that will help you establish your legitimacy. In our society, where money is so greatly respected for what it can get you as a means to all things buyable, there is certain to be an attraction between, and a yearning in pariah people for, wealth and money.

The police have long exhibited this money yearning. Police corruption may, in part, be a fact of this yearning. Corruption tends to be exampled in the taking of bribes and under-the-table payoffs, usually in the areas of vice activities, drugs, gambling, and prostitution. Once again, it is the ghetto where most of these activities are thought to be rampant. Police corruption tends to be common to the urban ghettos.

Also, it should be mentioned that this yearning for money takes the legitimate form of collective bargaining by police unions. Police yearning for money is not then only a factor of lower-middle-class policemen needing money to keep up an appearance, a private lifestyle, it is also needed to give them an emotional sense of anchoring in a society where they frequently feel cut adrift. The money yearning for the police is also a factor that causes them to be more mercenary about their job. Money helps to justify the ghetto cops being in that downtrodden community.

Mercenaries, by their name, were social, cultural outsiders. They involved themselves in others' affairs without a commitment to the cultural life of the host society they tended to fight for; nor did they involve themselves in the social environment where they displayed their fighting talents. It could be said then that mercenaries were, by the social role they played, pariahs. Mercenaries were usually the toughest soldiers, and they were used in the toughest sector of the fighting. Our society views the ghetto as the toughest sector of the fight against crime. We have not forgotten that the sixties showed us that the ghetto housed the enemy.

It would seem that pariah people would make good rule enforcers. They have no personal ties, or at least less ties, to traditional values and the traditional way of life, and therefore they can enforce the rules because they are the rules, without any necessary commitment to the waning or strengthening of the values that gave rise to the rules. Certainly, the policeman is a member of this society in the broad sense, but in the ghetto he is a social entity apart from that cultural life. Therefore, the rules they enforce tend not to be basic to the ghetto society, but rather they are an outgrowth of the larger society.

Being a rule enforcer helps to give social meaning to the existence of a pariah people. Here they can be promulgating the social reality of the mainstream and to that degree they can attach themselves to it. They can promulgate the rules while not feeling they necessarily have to take responsibility for them. So the pariah status of the police worked very well during the turmoil of the sixties when the police were used to protect civil rights marchers, protect young black children who were integrating all white schools, and helping blacks secure their rights to vote in the segregated South. But during that period, the police were also being used to decimate the Black Panthers, ruthlessly and unrelentingly, and to attack the anti-war demonstrators. The more they enforce the rules without value judgments, the more secure the pariah people are likely to feel in the society.

Floating like flotsam and jetsam, the pariah feels the urgency to justify his position, and he desperately wants to win the respect of those who are accepted as normal in the society. In the ghetto his position is justified by carrying out the will of society, that is, being attendant over the ghetto institution. And he tries to win the respect of the residents there by alternately meeting their social service needs, and demonstrating to them that he is an authority which represents mainstream values. In a very personal sense, the police officer pariah presents himself as a person of higher status in the larger society that controls the lesser society of the ghetto.

Pariah people are rejected people, yet they are a needed people. The need may be as much psychosomatic as functionally necessary to the basic operations of the society, but a need nevertheless. Undoubtedly it becomes difficult for a group to identify with a society that repels them. In the ghetto the police are repelled as an ongoing fact of that community's existence. It becomes confusing as to who the pariah people might identify with. There is always the subculture, for the pariah, for the police. That remains constant, and society seems to prefer a subculture status for the pariah because he is not a social member in the best of standings. He is looked down upon, even though the social rhetoric from the mainstream attempts to give a different appearance to this view.

JUDAS GOATS

The policemen in the ghetto are social brokers, and as such they are responsible for providing certain social services for the people of that community. Indeed, it is that none of the other social brokers, the teachers, welfare case workers, probation officers, and the like give as much of their time to administering direct social services to the ghetto community as do the police. Most of the work of the police in the ghetto is social work, contrary to what is generally believed. The police perform a great many noncriminally oriented services as well.

The police stay busy in the ghetto taking the sick to hospitals, settling domestic quarrels, searching for lost children, directing traffic, guarding school crossings, and doing many other services like directing people to the right kinds of social services that can deal with their problems. The ghetto is most active in the evening and on the weekends. It is most active at the times when social agencies, public or private, are closed. This means, in effect, that the police are providing essential services that would go unmet were they not available.

There is rarely the cry of "offing the pig" when the cop is providing needed social services. By the same token, the police do not seem to be hampered by fears of endangerment from the black community when they are delivering those services. Of course, when people are in need they will reach out to fulfill it in whatever way they can and worry about the consequences later. Policemen are known to speak of themselves as individuals who have a passion for helping others. If what they say is true, it is a basic part of their personalities. Need and passion overcome the adversary quality of police-community relations. Or are the social service functions of the police consistent with their role in the ghetto? This question should actually be seen in light of the fact that within the confines of the police role in the ghetto, dichotomous social relations are not necessarily incompatible.

Regardless of the social services provided by the police in the ghetto, we have already spoken of the many negative affects that the police have on the ghetto community. Because of this it is difficult to believe that policemen do their social work because of an honest beneficence for ghetto residents. Why, the police are not even given much credit for their social work activities. Their commanders and the public care about arrest records, "the collars" that are made. Time spent directly helping people is likely to be played down when the department is justifying the reason for its existence.

The social work activities of the police in the ghetto probably have little to do with the police genuinely caring about the people in that community. Anthony Bouza, a former police commander in the borough of the Bronx in New York City, which happens to contain the worst ghetto in the entire city, may be able to offer us some insight into the role of the police in the ghetto. Bouza talks about the ghetto being filled with "feral children" that have been created by a society that manufactures an underclass of failures and pacifies them with welfare, TV and cheap liquor.[4]

If we accept Bouza's line of thinking, it is quite clear that the police social service activities in the ghetto are but just another aspect of the pacification of the underclass. Bouza implies as much when he says, "Crime is a symptom in this society, and the disease is poverty. As a policeman I could do little about the disease but comment on it. I was paid to attack the symptoms."

Solving or attempting to solve the ghetto's many social problems is not a police responsibility, nor am I saying that it should be. However, no matter what acts they perform, the basic nature of police work remains political in an overall policy sense. It is our society as a whole which deems it necessary to have an underclass, and likewise it is our society which deems a policy of pacification that requires the police to be providers of social services to the human junk heaps. Pacification, as a social policy, is a policy of containment. Pacification is a means of neutralizing discontent, a way of trying to win over people who might otherwise be adversaries.

Pacification, by its nature, is manipulative, devious, and underhanded. It is a practice that was much used by conquerors and colonizers over subjected people. Services, help, and support are rendered to the people, in the smallest quantity allowable, not for the sake and concern of the people, but for the sake and concern of controlling them.

Anthony Bouza's reference to the feral children of the ghetto is no different than the more widespread police comment of the ghetto being filled with jungle bunnies; nor is it much different than saying that blacks practice life much nearer to its primordial psychobiological baseline, and in the final analysis the references give credence to the fact that the police probably see blacks as borderline primitives.

Feral children are wild children. Francois Truffaut pointed this out in his film *The Wild Child.* You cannot reason with the wild child. Rational explanation, normal human habits of fellow-respect, concern and decency in dealing with others, and just a normal state of civility and manners are thought to be impossible with a feral individual. But what is even worse, feral children tend to be very aggressive and physical in the manner in which they attempt to deal with their environment and specifically, when they are trying to solve problems. Feral children cannot be changed. The feral young person becomes a feral adult, all the while remaining an immature, highly emotional child. And since they cannot be changed, they must be looked after, attended to in an environment that separates them from the normal population.

Our society has a very strict policy that wild creatures that live among us must be strictly attended to, and more often than not they must be kept in an institution like the zoo, or kept under constant surveillance like in a circus. We have great fears that if these wild creatures are not treated thusly, they may easily attack us or run amok in the populace hurting, if not killing, people. Are feral children in the same category as those other wild creatures like lions, tigers, and bears? Did you know that sightseeing buses regularly go up to Harlem, carrying out-of-towners who stare out of stained glass windows and gawk at the residents?

When the wild creatures within our midst refuse to be pacified and

and controlled any longer then we put them out of their misery. We put them to sleep. There is the case of the elephant who had been a long-term resident of the Central Park Zoo in New York. Suddenly, for no reason that his keepers and attendants could understand, the animal became intolerant of his incarcerated lifestyle. The creature began to revert to a wild state by attacking the people who fed it, and the visitors who came to stare and feed it peanuts and crackerjacks through the cage bars. It was finally determined that the elephant was incorrigible and had to be put to sleep. Death was administered by *drugs*.

There are those observers of the ghetto who say that drugs have played a very significant role in the history of the ghetto. These same observers say that drugs are very important to police work in the ghetto. Samuel F. Yette says that the police have long encouraged the spread of heroin in the ghetto (and now methadone) because it helps to pacify and control the community.[5] Commander Bouza says that alcohol is also used in this way. Looking back to the 1960s, drugs played a significant role in the outcome of the ghetto protest, says Yette. The potential revolutionaries in the ghetto, the street people, were torn apart from within by heroin. It was those individuals who would have been the heaviest mother-fuckers in town, who might have been fighting cops or creating unrest, who are now desperately killing and stealing from each other in order to feed their habits. This is how the ghetto is controlled. This is how Harlem, Watts, and Philadelphia's black areas are kept impotent. It is also one of the main reasons why Haight-Ashbury was changed from one of the finest places in the country to go and free yourself into a ghetto where, in the first months of 1970, there were twenty-four murders, many deaths from disease, girls raped, and freaks beaten. The threat of the Haight was dealt with.

Drugs were heavy in the ghettos of this nation for years. The police and all responsible authorities who had reason to know it, knew it. We heard it being said that as long as it was in the ghetto it was alright because no one cared about the blacks who were getting high on smack. And if it wasn't smack, then they were sure to be getting high on booze. This is just the way those people are. You can't blame it on the police because the blacks dig smack. Yes, it is fairly well known that the shit the cops confiscate in busts tends to find its way back onto the streets. Just recall the well-publicized bust in *The French Connection*. The whole cache disappeared from the police station. Yes, the police generally, if not almost entirely, bust small-time drug hustlers. They never seem to touch the big cheese. It is the big cheese who is at the bottle neck. He has to keep the smack flowing, but if you pick off a little pusher way down at the end of the line, then he really cannot interfere with the flow of the goods. The police know this, like everyone else. Alright! Alright! But the police do not use drugs in their work in the black community. Oh yeah! Dig this!

Smack also provides the police with the best of special informants and agents, people from the community itself. A narcotics detective catches some strung-out cat with dope on him, takes him to the precinct, gets all the names he can squeeze out of him, scares him to death, then turns him loose, giving him some smack for the road. The cat is now an informer, and if he won't come across when asked, he'll be busted. Therefore, the cat keeps giving names, and the cops may have him set up deals, giving him most of the dope from the new busts. There are countless tales of people being busted with hundreds of dollars worth of dope on them, only to come into court and hear the cops tell the judge that they found just enough dope for scientific analysis and conviction.

Using drugs to manipulate, to pacify, and control is nothing new in the relationship between oppressor and oppressed. Drugs are a unique element for this task because of the high, the feeling of unreality, and the hallucinatory nature of the experience. One is seemingly being given an enjoyment while the problems of being oppressed become dull and dim to the senses. This tool of oppression comes on as a protection, an insulation to oppression. And, because the hard drugs are habit forming, the junkie then becomes the chief tool of his own oppression. Nothing could be more efficient for the oppressor. This fact becomes extremely important when you are dealing with large numbers of people. The destruction of the addict is administered by the junkie's own hand.

Culturally, Americans identify with the British more than any other people in the world. We copy their mannerisms. We imitate their style. The British knew the importance of drugs when trying to control large populations. They were masters at pacifying and dominating unwilling peoples.

Using heroin or other opiates to destroy the will of oppressed people has been historically authenticated as an imperialist tool. The British introduced the Chinese to opiates in the last century, and then spread the myth that opium came from China. The British imported it from India and Turkey for the purpose of stringing out the Chinese and bringing them under the control of the empire. The Chinese had rebelled with the support of their empress and eventually were defeated in the "Opium Wars." The animosity of the Chinese for Westerners culminated in the Boxer Rebellion which was crushed by the nine imperial powers, including the United States. The drug traffic was not driven out of China until 1949 when that country was totally decolonized of western European presence.

The police in the ghetto, as urban colonial guards, are there in part to see that decolonization does not take place in any form. Take the case of Chicago's famous and infamous Blackstone Rangers of the 1960s. This group, also known as the Black P Stone Nation (the "P" stands for black "princes") came to be publicly known as the largest and perhaps most feared street gang Chicago, or even the nation, had ever known. In the 1960s, they numbered in the thousands, their dangerous turf stretching from the far South Side to north of the Loop.

In the police records, it says that they came up with the idea of using juveniles as junior hit men, the theory being that juveniles would not be prosecuted for murder. But at the same time, the Blackstone Rangers managed to be funded, indirectly, by the federal government to the tune of hundreds of thousands of dollars (a fact which helped to turn the establishment against the poverty program). Also they received tens of thousands of dollars, by police count, from millionaires seeking to lend a hand to what they thought were the deserving poor. And it does seem strange that if the Blackstone Rangers were getting all this legal money, they would then have to resort to the magnitude of crimes that the police records indicate.

Nevertheless, it was not the money or crime of the Blackstone Rangers that scared the hell out of the Chicago police and the establishment in America. It was the power that this black group amassed in a ghetto neighborhood, power that was taking the reins of control away from the institutional attendants. This power was clearly exampled on July 8, 1968, when thousands of Blackstone Rangers staged a march on Chicago's South Side to meet their adversaries, the Disciples.

It was a hot afternoon on 63rd Street in the spring of 1968, and the word was out that the "Stones" (Blackstone Rangers), would march on the Midway. The Midway, a wide green promenade area three blocks south of 63rd Street, got its name because it was the midway of Chicago's 1892 Columbian Exposition. Today, it separates grimy and primitive Woodlawn from the austere gothic front of the University of Chicago.

As the day wore on, there was little indication of a march. All that was to be seen along the midway were about twenty or so black youths milling around at the west end of the strip. There were almost as many nervous Chicago policemen watching them. But suddenly a distant thunder stirred north on Ellis Avenue. And then they came, down Ellis Avenue ten abreast, ghetto kids with their fists in the air, breaking into a run, and the police unable or unwilling to stop them. The youths were shouting "Black-stone! Black-stone!"

Two contingents of Stones, from different directions, met on the Midway that day and marched. There were thousands upon thousands of them, marching to the chant of "Black-stone." They all marched to meet one man, Jeff Fort, one of the original founders of the Blackstone Rangers. It was a show of power, of command and control.

The police said the Blackstone Rangers were nothing but thugs, hoodlums, and gangsters. But John Fry, pastor of the venerable First Presbyterian Church where the Blackstone Rangers had their headquarters, said, "Malcolm X should have lived long enough to see it. . . .To be a Ranger was to be really black for the first time. . . . A nation was born." The Stones were a solid group, says Fry in his book *Locked-Out Americans,* because a Stone would not "renounce his being as a prince in order to resume his being a nigger kid."

However, by 1972 the Blackstone Rangers had cracked wide open. The organization collapsed. What happened to them? Commander Thomas Hughes of the Chicago police gang unit was reported to have said in May of 1978 that the Stones were dead, and it was the Chicago police who put them out of business. Hughes said, "Their hard core is dead or in prison or junkies." As the police tell it, the Stones started dying when leaders of their "Main 21," Jeff Fort and Eugene "Bull" Hairston went to jail on assorted charges and took their discipline, criminal expertise, and charisma with them. "The structure broke down," the policeman said, "when the Stones found themselves free to plunder on their own, and they became greedy, plunged into the narcotics trade, and stepped up killing each other."

That is the police version of what happened to the Stones, but an old Blackstone Ranger of fifteen years with the group had another version to tell:

The Stones didn't disintegrate. The leadership, the Main 21, that's the only one. It can be said that the police had a definite association with that. They tried to make addicts out of them. They used the leadership.

Drugs were made available and those of us who resisted, they would get killed. A lot of them got killed for resisting and they were killed by police. . . .[6]

The police come to the ghetto with the societal image of the good guys, the protectors of law and order, the protectors of the little guy. They are still largely righteous symbols to be emulated. In the poorer and less affluent neighborhoods PAL activities are popular ways that the police maintain their image[7] and advocate the needs of the ghetto community they may serve. And specific to the ghetto, the police are the chief means of providing social services to the community. Without such services, it is quite likely that there would be little or no social equilibrium in the community. Without such services there would be a growing tide of unmet needs that could build until the frustrations, the hurt, and pain erupt, i.e., the riots of the sixties. The police provision of social services helps to keep the people in the ghetto pacified. Residents look to the police for services because they have no alternative after five o'clock and on the weekends. The normal social service agencies are closed down at those times.

For the police, pacification is a double-edged sword. They will be helpful or they will be harmful to the ghetto community. It is all the same thing. If helping sick people go to the hospital will keep the ghetto cool, then that will be a normal part of the police role in the black neighborhoods. If socking drugs to the leaders of powerful gangs or community groups will keep the ghetto cool, then it is within the normal responsibilities of rule enforcers and the social brokers.

To be sure, the ultimate form of social broking is in the form of decisions that decide who shall live and who shall die. When drugs are turned loose in communities or are allowed to persist there, this is that kind of decision. Members of the Blackstone Rangers probably found this out the hard way.

The police, if I may paraphrase Commander Bouza, are being required to lead the feral flock. They are to lead them deeper into the ghetto. Are the police not Judas Goats?

SACRIFICIAL LAMBS

When Commander Anthony Bouza says that he was "paid to attack the symptoms" of poverty, along with addressing pacification he is also inadvertently giving recognition to the fact that the problems of crime and the causes of crime go far beyond the policeman's ability to solve them. Collaring criminals will not prevent crime. As we have noted, the sociological theories on deviancy say that crime is a result of poverty and poor socioeconomic conditions. As long as there is poverty, there will be crime. Black ghettos in America are just another name for poverty. And if we follow this logic then ipso facto, high crime rates in the ghetto. By this conclusion alone, police action in the ghetto could be nothing more than a holding action.

Over the last four years, the crime rates in the major cities of the nation have been declining. It is a small decline, but it is significant because crime rates in the large cities increased steadily from 1965-1974.[8] This would seem to indicate that the police are catching the criminals and preventing crimes. The police are doing the job that society asked of them. But are they? The public does not view the police as doing a good job. Most

Americans now believe that the police are not doing an effective job.[9] The police should be doing more to protect the citizen from the mugger, the rapist, the murderer. The public keeps exhorting the police to do more, even though crime is dropping and poverty is worsening in the ghetto due to "stagflation" and growing unemployment.

The police respond to this exhortation by saying that they are sorely outnumbered by the criminals, burdened with responsibilities that should be performed by social workers, and tremendously handicapped by a criminal justice system that cares more for the rights of the criminal than it cares for the rights of the victim or the law enforcement officer.

Then, there are the logistics of the crime problem that can only exacerbate the difficulties of the police efforts. Take New York City, for example: the three major boroughs of the city, Manhattan, Brooklyn, and the Bronx have teeming, stagnated, impoverished ghettos. Most of the city's crime, according to statistics, occurs in these ghettos and their surrounding districts. In an average year in New York City, there are more than 1,000 murders (the actual figure for 1977 was 1,557 murders, 1,622 in 1976), [10] 1,300 rapes, 15,000 burglaries, 10,000 auto thefts, 12,000 felonious assaults, and 19,000 robberies. For a 25,000 member force, the New York City police make almost a quarter of a million arrests a year, which is about one arrest every two minutes.

These statistics are awesome in terms of spelling out the amount of crime that is occurring in New York City. However, there is another important piece of information that needs to be added to these statistics. The Justice Department in Washington estimates that for each serious criminal act that is reported throughout the nation, two others are not.[11] This probably means that the actual amount of serious crime being committed in New York City is far beyond the ability of the police force to cope with. And, this may further suggest that the New York City police force, more than fighting crime, has come to coexist with it.

In the ghetto, this coexisting can exact a terrible price on the police officer. It is unreal for society to believe that he can face the raw human suffering in that community, day after day, and not be deeply affected by it. No matter where a cop is assigned, police work is high-intensity, high–stress work. In New York City, about forty cops each year are pensioned out of the police department because of mental and drinking problems that prohibit them from carrying guns or doing regular precinct duty, and about three hundred officers have their guns taken away from them temporarily for the same problems each year.[12]

Emotionally and psychologically, the working cop in the ghetto is only a little better off than the people he must watch over. For if the truth be known, he has become a throwaway too in a throwaway society, and ultimately his psyche becomes damaged in ways similar to the ghetto resident. This occurs not because he is a Johnny-do-gooder or a bleeding heart liberal, but rather because in time he becomes aware of a basic fact— that he has been co-opted, willingly to be sure, by a social system that, in effect, requires him to be both a *Judas Goat* and a *Sacrificial Lamb*.

Be a member of New York's finest? Help people! Protect society from the criminals, the deviants! That is what the propaganda said. But what it did not say was that the police officer in the ghetto is likely to become a deviant himself in order to play his policeman's role. If nothing else, he will surely develop a schizoid personality. Why? Because on the one hand, as the social worker, he will be required to lead the feral flock, but on the other hand, as a law enforcement agent, he will have to be suspicious of his followers and to that degree, fearful of and unfaithful to them.

Also the propaganda does not make the point clear that the ghetto policeman has to be tough in the rugged individualist and frontiersman sense. He will be stationed at one of the society's outposts, and he shall be called upon to plot, scheme, coerce, threaten, and use physical force against ghetto residents—all in the performance of his duty. The same duty, at times, may cause him to kill, and be in jeopardy of being killed. The ghetto policeman will inevitably learn to think and even act like a criminal when the need arises. That is the way to get collars, but it is also a matter of survival.

As colonial guards, policemen pride themselves on being tough, abusive, and using force against small time, ghetto hoods. The guards pride themselves on their knowledge and awareness of the community where they serve, and they tend to take advantage of their authority in getting the job done. The TV characters of Kojak and Barreta, played by Telly Savalas and Robert Blake are perfect examples of the hard-nosed colonial guards. At times, their behavior is indistinguishable from the crooks they are trying to catch on the weekly TV series, and the distinction is deliberately blurred because society wants to keep its option open to withdraw support from colonial guards whenever their behavior becomes an embarrassment to the system. Clint Eastwood's *Dirty Harry* is another one of these rugged guard types.

In the 1960s, it became feasible for politicians, big city mayors like John Lindsay of New York, to support police civilian review boards. These boards were a way in which politicians were willing to withdraw support from the police because of the ways the police were handling civil rights marchers and anti-war demonstrators in such a blatantly unconstitutional and brutal manner. Police behavior had become an embarrassment to the system. The colonial guard had been given free reign in the ghetto for a hundred years, but when the actions of the guards were caught on newsreel film for the American public and the world to see—the smashing of heads and the busting of backs—the exposure was too much to tolerate without some compensation for sociopolitical balance. America still had an image to maintain. However, this is to suggest how expendable are the urban colonial guard. They will be thrown to the jungle bunnies, so to speak, whenever it is politically expedient to do so.

For many white Americans, the ghetto is not filled with people, but it is filled with a disease, a disease of nonwhiteness. It is a communicable disease, therefore its carriers must be isolated and separated from the rest of society. Whites must be very careful to not allow this disease to infiltrate their neighborhoods, on school buses or buying the house next door. And anyone who works ongoingly with the disease must be suspected because the disease is infectious. Remember how the middle-class white kids went to the ghettos in the sixties to help out the wretched poor and were tainted with some of that nonwhiteness we call drug addiction? At least that is what James Q. Wilson tells us. But what about police corruption that tends to be a hallmark of the police who work in the ghettos? The 1972 Knapp Commission in New York City told us all about that.

But the infection is much more subtle than the effects of drugs or police corruption. That is what makes it so deadly. It eats at one's moral and ethical fabric. Since 1974 the New York City Police Department has had an Ethical Awareness Workshop program that is mandatory for all officers through the rank of lieutenant.[13] This program gives recognition to the moral and ethical debasement that can so easily, and so readily overtake a policeman in his job. More than four thousand officers a year attended the program until it was cut back in the spring of 1978.

The policemen who work in the ghetto are seen as being different by policemen who do not work in the ghetto, and by the policemen of ghetto precincts themselves. Officers who do not work in the ghetto look at officers who do as men who have been assigned to the worst duty stations in the city. Such assignments can be for punishment, although in New York City this is generally not the case. The movie *Serpico* is a case in point. Serpico was transferred to a tough precinct because of his persistent allegations about corruption in the police department. Commanders in the New York City Police Department have been known to threaten officers with the statement that if they did not shape up they would be transferred out of Staten Island or Queens to Harlem, Bedford Stuyvesant, or the South Bronx. These are all ghetto areas of the city.

Policemen who work in the ghetto tend to be seen as more tense and secretive by other officers. This may be due to the fact that ghetto policemen do work in the most active precincts of a city in terms of arrests, social work activity, and troubleshooting. But the fact that they are seen differently means that they tend to draw more into themselves. This holds true in any event since police officers tend to segregate themselves in terms of their friends and associations along the lines of their precinct assignments. Policemen of the same precinct tend to befriend each other and hang out together.

It is expected that policemen who work in the most active, most crime-ridden precincts will inevitably face the most danger ongoingly. That is their fate because that is their job, and like Serpico, some of those guys are working in those high-crime districts for reasons that have nothing to do with the normal assignment process. When you face the music, there are times when you will have to pay the piper.

The policemen of the ghetto have a strong attachment and camaraderie for each other. The high rate of confrontation with danger makes them very dependent upon each other. They tend to see themselves as society's bulwark against crime, lawlessness, and disorder. Without their services, they believe that society could not survive against the onslaught of the deviant. This attitude was clearly exampled in the name given to a precinct in the South Bronx of New York City: "Fort Apache!"

The officers of the ghetto precincts become accustomed to the excitement and activity of their beats. They tend to look down on those officers who work in the slow precincts as do–nothings and shirkers. After a few years in a ghetto precinct, the policemen do not want to work any place else because they believe they would be bored by the inactivity, and because they believe that they are doing the real police work. This is to suggest that the policemen of the ghetto can feel very altruistic about their job and very moral in their dedication to it.

Policemen in the ghetto, as perhaps policemen in all communities of society, face danger because they feel it is their duty to do so. By the same token, they face danger because they think nothing will happen to them. "If I thought I was going to get killed, then I wouldn't stay on this job. I'm not a crazy nut." Yet, policemen are killed on the job in the line of duty each year. They believe that the sacrifice will ultimately result in the betterment of society, and therefore when a policeman is killed doing his duty, his death may be, in Emile Durkheim's words, a form of "altruistic suicide."[14]

We thus confront a type of suicide differing by incisive qualities from the preceding one. Whereas the latter is due to excessive individuation, the former is caused by too rudimentary individuation. One occurs because society allows the individual to escape it, being insufficiently aggregated in some parts or even in the whole; the other, because society holds him in too strict tutelage. Having given the name of egoism to the state of the ego living its own life and obeying itself alone, that of *altruism* adequately expresses the opposite state, where the ego is not its own property, where it is blended with something not itself, where the goal of conduct is exterior to itself, that is, in one of the groups in which it participates. So we call the suicide caused by intense altruism *altruistic suicide.* But since it is also characteristically performed as a duty, the terminology adopted should express this fact. So we will call such a type obligatory altruistic suicide.[15]

Altruism is important particularly to the psychology of policemen who work in the ghetto. Police officers are there not because they care about the residents per se; nor are they principally there for ego fulfillment. They are there because it is obligatory with the job, and perhaps as a result of their earlier Protestant upbringing. It is quite possible for policemen to work in white middle-class neighborhoods where they identify very strongly with the community and the people. To the extent that cops accept the obligations of their jobs, which call upon them to put their lives in jeopardy when needed, the job dictates their individual life's fate. In higher crime districts of the cities, this dictation is much stronger because the probability of mortal danger is much more likely.

To state the case more simply, because of the responsibilities police officers assume when they put on their uniforms, some of them are expected to die. If they work in the ghetto they are expected to die more often because they are the lambs who guard the feral flock. Because the obligatory command to duty is stronger in the ghetto, it accelerates the possibilities of altruistic suicide.

When a policeman dies in the line of duty, he is honored more in death than he would ever be in life. He is given a full inspector's funeral. His fellow officers will come out in the hundreds, along with the police commissioner and very likely the mayor, to pay their last respects. And he is likely to be eulogized as someone who died helping and caring for his fellow man. His comrades may speak of the sorrow now that the deceased is gone. His death was a tragedy. Yet, each officer who would stand at the funeral of a dead colleague knows that the dead officer practically signed his death warrant when he put the blue uniform on. Policemen are expected to die tragically in service to their society. What we want to know each year is not why they die, but how they die. And of course, we want to know how many have died.

A policeman's blue uniform attracts death, true enough. The sentiment of off the pig has not yet completely died away in the ghetto. At the same time, it is the ghetto which gives the policemen reasons and rationalizations for the wearing and presence of that uniform in society. "The ghetto is a community of institutionalized deviancy and society must be

protected from it." The disease of nonwhiteness must be kept behind
ghetto walls, and for this effort to succeed, policemen must make the
ultimate sacrifice again, and again, and again, and again.

COOL COP

After a time, the cop working in the ghetto comes to realize that the
problems that confront him in totality cannot be solved with a nightstick
and a gun. To be sure, the police have to struggle just to cope with the
crime in the area. Most importantly, as Commander Douza points out,
it is society that manufactures an underclass of failures and pacifies them
with welfare, TV, and cheap liquor. In this respect then, the larger society
is responsible for the problems of the ghetto, and it is the larger society
that will have to solve these problems. But until that time, the psyches and
bodies of police officers will be thrown on this human scrapheap to
appease a frightened society.

The policeman of the ghetto comes to see himself as just another
one of society's machines, cranked up to do a job and play out a self-
fulfilling prophesy in an environment of social degradation. He therefore
becomes emotionally detached from his work, cool, efficient, and
machinelike. He becomes a *cool cop*.

The notion of cool cop bespeaks of the withdrawal by the officer of
his caring, concern, commitment, and interest in the people, the community he works in. This characteristic was described very well by
Solomon Gross in his discussion of New York's Twenty-Third Precinct
in East Harlem. The policemen of that East Harlem precinct did not mix
socially with the people in that community. They complained about the
problems of the neighborhood, but their concern was usually passive. As
far as the police were concerned, it was the residents' responsibility to
correct the ills of their community, and finally, when the work day was
over, the officers quickly left the scene.

The emotionally detached attitude can also be seen in the incessant,
obsessive talk by police officers about their retirement. There is this need
to be futuristic in outlook which is a clear way to blank out, or attempt
to blank out, present surroundings and circumstances. The fact that this
type of conversation serves other purposes can be seen in that most
police officers find it very difficult to retire from the force after they
have put in twenty or thirty years of service. And if they have spent much
of that time in the ghetto as their place of work, retirement can even be
harder. The motion picture *The New Centurions* with George C. Scott and
Stacy Keach cinematically exposed this type of problem. The excitement

of exposing oneself to danger for many years is impossible to replace in retirement.

The New Centurions was also interesting because it showed the attempts of older police officers to get younger police officers to be more impersonal, machinelike, and efficient in the performance of their duties. A certain detachment, even among brother officers, was thought to be a good thing for policemen. If an officer gets killed, you are less likely to take it so hard if you have kept some emotional distance between you and your comrades. However, since policemen generally work in pairs, it is very difficult to keep this kind of emotional distance between working partners.

A cool cop behavioral attitude would seem to be an outgrowth of the situation the policeman finds when working in the ghetto. This would suggest that it is probably a circumstantial development rather than a function of society's overall relations with the ghetto. However, the cool cop attitude just happens to be very much suited to the overall police functions in that community. To be emotionally detached is a plus in terms of the police being rule enforcers, social brokers, colonial guards, and stratiphiles. As marginal men, they have the feelings and rationalizations to support these behaviors. Being detached allows the police to be more critical and objective in carrying out their social mandate in the ghetto.

In the last three or four decades, being cool, which is to say being impersonal and efficient, has become somewhat of an ideal for the police. This has resulted from the desire of the police to have their occupation seen as a profession. The wish for professional status is very much an outgrowth of bureaucratic organizational techniques coming to control the administrative mechanisms of government, and in particular, police departments. Bureaucracy stresses impersonality, efficiency, and behavior by administrative rules rather than behavior by feelings and emotions.

It is interesting to note that as the professional attitude has become more desirable, the ghetto has grown in its importance to police departments. The ghetto has become the chief means by which the police justify their existence, their huge budgets, their army of officers. Most of their statistics come from the ghetto. In bureaucratese, the cool cop is a more efficient cop, which means he is doing a better job on the streets. Doing a better job means for the police bureaucracy that he is generating more statistics which the department needs to help define its existence. Bureaucracy then encourages the cool cop behavior.

With municipal budgets decreasing all across the country, and city governments seeking ways to be more efficient with less, the cool cop behavior will take on, very likely, even greater importance in the future.

Therefore, the behavior of the ghetto cop may spread the cool, withdrawn attitude, into middle class and other nonghetto precincts more so than in the past. To be sure, as police departments continue their hardening of the administrative arteries, rigidifying their command structure, police behavior will be required to become more and more cool-like wherever the officers work.

The growing force of bureaucracy in police departments and society at large, means greater demands for organizational behavior throughout society wherever police work. This is likely to mean that the police will increasingly see themselves as separated from the traditional communities where they serve. The ghetto would be a standout in this relationship As a consequence, the police will probably fall back more and more on their subculture network. Being a cool cop is consistent with being a member of a select subculture like the police.

As the policemen develop their behavior of being cool cops, they act out more and more the role of the bureaucrat. The ghetto inadvertently nurtures this role. It is not surprising then that ghetto cops tend to cling strongly to their rules and develop the problems that can come with working by a rule-book mentality. In this context, the police are an extension of a bureaucratic mechanism, the police department, but generally they come to represent the bureaucratic world that oversees the social reality of the ghetto residents, much more so than say, the teachers, social workers, or parole and probation officers.

The police serve as the means of pulling the jungle bunnies back towards societal mainstream values, and these values have become shaped by bureaucratic mechanisms. Police are then instruments of bureaucratic penetration into local communities, and they bring with them certain values that if adopted by the local residents can only be a source of disfigurement and non-communal spirit among the people. Yet, as role models through their recognized position in our stratified society and through PAL, for instance, the police come as value-laden actors to the ghetto community. Since the values being presented are a source for fractioning community relations and spirit, it would be only natural for the people to resist it. Here is yet another reason for the resident to be noncooperative with the police.

There are a number of problems that result directly from working by a rule-book mentality. One such problem is the development of a routine, or a series of routines in one's work. This occurs from having special times for coffee breaks and taking naps on the late shifts, to the manner in which certain police calls are handled and the methods that are used to avoid being trapped in work that will carry over beyond the end of the shift. Not only are there routines developed for certain types of police calls, but they are also developed for dealing with certain types and classes of people, which is very consistent with the stratiphilian attitudes of police officers.

Therefore, a routine is developed for handling family disputes. It is a routine that permits only minimal personal involvement. And there is the routine for drunks—leave them be if they are not making a public nuisance of themselves—for kids standing around on the corners being noisy and drinking beer—let them be unless they are making a loud, public nuisance of themselves. And on and on it goes, routines for avoiding contact and involvement with the residents, except at an impersonal distance.

However, routinization of any social process has its own built-in problems. It will bring boredom to the functions routinized, and the boredom will cause the person to become even less caring about the routines. But even more difficult is the fact that the routinization produces a noncreative posture in the work and it becomes bereft of a sense of aesthetic reward. The police officer does not attribute his boredom and lack of aestheticism to the routines that he uses to conduct his behavior. On the contrary, the ghetto is held responsible for the unrewarding nature of police work.

Impersonality is a major problem. Professionalization calls upon it. Efficiency seems to demand it. Yet it lessens a caring for the job and work in personal terms. The police officer looks at his work for what it can do for him, in terms of salary, prestige, and that ever-loving pension. This brings on a very utilitarian attitude. Clearly this has been shown to be the case in the last decade or more, when policemen have had struggles with municipalities over increased salaries. Police benevolent associations have become powerful political organizations because of their increased role as union agents for their police officer members, who are not opposed to threatening and going out on strike if they do not get what they want from city governments in contract negotiations.

The utilitarian attitude tends to be seen by the police in the actions of other social groups, in effect saying to the police that the groups are competing with them. This is particularly true in the eyes of groups that are dependent upon the same resources as the policemen themselves. They see the firemen as competing with them for salary resources, and they can also see the residents of the ghetto as competing with them because the residents are on welfare; that is, on the city's payroll. There is less to go around for the police with so many of those blacks on the dole.

The policeman's work habits are directed, if not governed by, rules and regulations of the highest secular, legitimizing authority. The rules direct police behavior towards goals like collaring criminals, reducing the crime rates, and enhancing the status of the department in the public's eyes. Without a genuine personal commitment, police officers can become attached to goals as a basis for rationalizing the work they do, and rationalizations need rational support.

The policeman can develop a certain tunnel vision about the importance of his work. He sees himself as doing one of the most important jobs in all of society, keeping the tide of anarchy and lawlessness from sweeping over mankind. It is this view that confirms his utilitarian attitude about his work. He becomes less able to see the contributions of others to the well-being of society. But even when he acknowledges the contributions of others, he will inevitably see himself as being part of the most important group.

This attachment to goals is also a way of keeping that future orientation. One is less likely to become involved in the environment around him when he is constantly looking to what will be rather than what is. The ghetto residents are also seen as being attached to their goals, the goals of organized deviancy and the perpetuation of a lifestyle on the dole. It is the lifestyle of the residents that puts them in a position of restraining if not preventing the attainment of the goals that the police have set for themselves as an organization. This sparks antagonism between the two groups, among many other antagonisms.

Tunnel vision links up to a form of narrowmindedness which relies upon the quick definition, the stereotype, or better still, categorization. This type of jadedness is directly related to the policeman's job, and it is a function of his belief that he is better than civilians in general because of his ability to make quick decisions and so on. In categorization, the individual defines his world by the terms of his job, the rules, the regulations, and even the slang and in-language of his vocational role.

For the policeman, the world is filled with only two categories, the victim and perpetrator. These categories easily get transferred to society at large in terms of seeing ghetto people as perpetrators and white middle-class people as victims. Of course, it is the policeman who must stand between the two with his finger in the dike. But people in general for the policeman become a list of law violations, the auto speeder, the second story man, the pusher, the bookie, the streetwalker, a film-flammer, a mugger, a rapist, a murderer. These categories lend themselves to easy use in the ghetto because the policeman feels he is in an alien environment. He can feel a little less uncomfortable with his situation if he can identify in broad terms the sea of humanity around him which he only relates to at a distance or when he must deal in some official category.

Certainly the result of this is to further increase the separation of the police from the people in the ghetto, and if the people are but a list of violations, then in some respects the ghetto community takes on a quality of being a function of the cop's job and the police department. Therefore, the police are made to feel that they can be as arbitrary, capricious, and cavalier as they like in the ghetto because the ghetto is there to serve their needs in good utilitarian fashion. Policemen are very likely then to take extraordinary liberties with the people of the ghetto or, to put it differently, use a great deal of discretion in working in that black community. Policemen feel they have a right, if not an obligation, to take these liberties to use their discretion, because only they really know and understand the people of the ghetto. It is a necessary way of wrenching respect from them for authority, and not only authority in terms of the blue uniform, but authority in terms of society as a whole.

Becoming wedded to rules and goals creates a resistance in the police against change. They resist change, for example, because they perceive it as interfering with their routines. Changes in work schedules and work assignments are to be resisted for this reason. Changes in administrations, new chiefs, and commissioners are also feared for the same reason. Unstable social environments, bohemian, skid row, ghetto areas easily perturb the police because instability portends change. This follows because the rules and regulations of the police invariably defend and protect the status quo. In fact this may be the chief goal of police work. When social change begins to alter traditional norms, the police can perceive this as being a direct threat to them. Social change challenges their sense of meaning and purpose in life.

For the police, the ghetto uprisings of the 1960s symbolized a general attack on the status quo. Blacks were acting completely out of character. They were not supposed to stand up to authority, and as the social brokers and colonial guards directly responsible for the blacks, the police took this behavior as being a direct affront and assault upon them and their rules and goals. Consequently, they forcibly and viciously resisted the blacks, cheered on by society's call to keep the enemy in the ghetto.

The cool cop with the rule-book mentality, acting out a detached role in the ghetto is aware of the fact that he is not in control of his job situation. There are his administrative masters, his commanders, and the state of crime and deviancy on the streets. The rule-book mentality has been developed in order to give commanders what they want. That is to say the cop deals with situations in a way to please his commanders. He does not want to buck the system nor make waves. In terms of the behavior of bureaucrats, this is a form of "ass-kissing."

This bureaucratic behavior, or form of ass-kissing, became directly linked to the ghetto in the 1960s. Ghetto residents were able to get a public and political hearing on the question of police brutality, and this occurred during the most heightened period of civil rights demonstrations. The police became very sensitive to criticism about their treatment of individuals from minority groups, and they became somewhat dependent on rule-book mentality in order to avoid accusations of brutality. This behavior was buttressed by Supreme Court decisions like *Mapp v. Ohio* and *Miranda v. Arizona* that further, say the police, tied their hands in dealing with the deviancy of the ghetto. And if this was not enough, police-community relations became a hot item in police departments, and civilian review boards came into vogue.

All of this led policemen to blame their rule-book mentality, their ass-kissing behavior on minorities, but principally on the blacks in the ghetto. For the ghetto folk, then, they will have a particular animus. It is one thing to be expected to kiss the ass of your commander, but it is another thing to be asked to kiss the ass of the public. Policemen with their stratiphilian outlook on society, and who work in the ghetto, can come to feel that their ass-kissing behavior requires them to kiss the "black asses" of the people in the ghetto. For a working cop, with a utilitarian outlook on the world, this attitude is intolerable. It makes the police want to explode sometimes, and that animosity may result in some bizarre behavior by policemen in the ghetto.

How can you care about people whose asses you are asked to kiss? It gives you a much better feeling to kick ass than to kiss it, if you're a cop

GHETTOIZED COP

The police officer who works in the ghetto is likely to become ghettoized. That is to say that the officer will come to feel rejected, abused, exploited, alienated, powerless, and a social throwaway all as a function of working in the ghetto. In recent years, cops, no matter where they worked, tended to feel rejected and abused by their public masters. It is one of the reasons they can feel contempt for the public. But, for the cop in the ghetto, being rejected is a direct result of working in the ghetto, and for cops in general, rejection is thought to result from the fact that they are just cops.

The public believes that the police are not doing a good job. If they were, the crime rates would not be so high. The public feels the police do their worst job in the ghetto, and the reason for this, is the fact that the ghetto cop has become a part of the criminal network that holds the ghetto together, as stated by Amitai Etzioni and in the findings of the Knapp Commission. Or more simply, it could be said that the public feels that if you're not a part of the solution then you must be part of the problem.

The policeman can feel rejected and abused because, as Commander Bouza puts it, "misplaced generosity" is one of our society's worst instincts. The policeman in the squalor of the ghetto, being urged to make the collar, wonders what the hell is going on when the perpetrators are let back out on the street as fast as a judge can give the order. But it is not only the courts that have become protective of the rights of the defendants, particularly as they might be reflected in the Miranda decision, there are also the prosecutors who of late have come to be the recipients of much ire from the police.

Police officers abhor the fact that even if they catch a criminal redhanded, it is still very likely that his punishment will not be commensurate with the gravity of the crime. Most criminal cases are settled through plea bargaining which invariably results in a lower sentence for the defendant. Why catch the crook if he is only going to be let out of jail? Prosecutors in New York City say that if they did not have plea bargaining the criminal justice system would collapse.

The scorn the police have for the courts can be seen in the name they gave to a New York City black judge, who they felt was letting criminals out of jail on bail and without bail when the accused should have been kept in jail or given a very high bail. They call the judge, "turn 'em loose Bruce." It so happens that this judge was releasing mostly poor blacks and Puerto Ricans, who, he said, did not have money for bail, and that their constitutional rights of presumption of innocence did not preclude the defendants being released in their own recognizance when the matter justified it.

These official acts of the criminal justice system that seem to fly in the face of the police are a source of making them feel alienated from the justice system of which they claim to be a part. This is a feeling that the ghetto folks have known all their lives. It makes the police and the ghetto residents feel powerless and manipulated. However, with the policemen's respect for authority, it is more likely that their frustration with the system will be turned not against the system but rather against elements outside it. In the case of the ghetto cops, they will direct their frustration towards those who seem to be causing their feelings of alienation. Are they being infected with the ghetto's disease, the disease of nonwhiteness?

In a very normal sense, the ghettoizing of the cop suits him well. That is to say, if he is to work in that community, he would best be served by being emotionally in tune with the environment. He would not accomplish much if he went about his job as though the ghetto were a white middle-class neighborhood or a Fifth Avenue beat. This fact serves society well because the police transmit the nature of their ghetto behavior to politicians, academicians, medical, and welfare personnel outside the ghetto for study, scrutiny, and understanding which helps the system deal with the ghetto. It is important to note that the police are a conduit and transmitter of information about the ghetto to other sources in the society. This is apart from crime and deviant statistics. We must not forget that very few people of the mainstream ever visit the ghetto. Our social vision of that community comes from the social brokers and the like who enter the ghetto on official business. As a part of this information-gathering mechanism, the police are the chief source because they spend so much time, and at all hours, in the ghetto. As well, the police tend to become intimately familiar with certain types of deviant behavior that greatly interest the public.

Police are thought to be experts on ghetto lifestyles. It matters not that their image of the ghetto may be very self-serving, since emphasizing crime in that community helps to justify their existence and enhance the police crime statistics. Indeed, it is the police who are specifically responsible for labeling the ghetto as a crime-ridden community of institutionalized deviancy. It was the social scientist who later picked up on this and attempted to justify it with his so-called scientific studies; which were little more than raising statistical correlations to confirm what police data had already suggested.

The police are a political tool and through manipulation of them by the politicians, through executive mandate and law, the system can practically get the police, in many ways, to produce the image of the ghetto it wants to parley to the public. Without police having close intimate ties to the ghetto, the cop being ghettoized, this would be more difficult to accomplish.

For years, through the 1940s and 1950s the police were sometimes advocates for the needs of less affluent kids through PAL and other activities. This meant that they were also being advocates for less affluent neighborhoods as a whole. The image being transmitted of the ghetto to the rest of society at that time was one of the unfortunate poor. Just recall those old-time 1930s movies of James Cagney and Pat O'Brien—the *Angels with Dirty Faces* type movies. The unfortunate poor was the message being given out there. These messages suggested that the police had the interests of the unfortunate poor at heart, and later the same message was very helpful to the civil rights movement in its earlier stages.

But then, in the sixties, the policemen came to be the spokesmen for all the crime, drugs, and disorder in the ghetto. They were delivering the message that the ghetto was a community of institutionalized deviancy.

The new image said that the ghetto society was not filled with the unfortunate poor, but rather it was filled with revolutionaries and criminals and drug addicts who wanted to overthrow our society. Poverty money, like that given to the Blackstone Rangers, for example, was being used to finance the overthrow of our system. Those crazy niggers had to be seen for what they really were.

Interestingly enough, it was at this time that the ideology of criminal justice came to be used, and law enforcement tied itself directly to the academicians in developing this new image of the ghetto. And as we have said earlier, the new wave academicians were into giving the ghetto a very poor image. Without the help of the academicians from big name schools, the ghetto image might not have been turned around as quickly as it was. But then, it should not be forgotten that the establishment of society wanted this new image, and the establishment was willing to pay millions and millions of dollars to academia to get this image firmly established in a hurry.

One of the main effects of ghettoization is the feeling in the person of being a prisoner in his community, but more so being a prisoner within himself. This feeling is one that comes from the person believing that he is not in control of the objective circumstances of his life. It is the feeling of Ralph Ellison's *Invisible Man,* that you do not belong to yourself, that you belong to someone else, that you are being manipulated, that you are just playing a role.

Yes, the cop in the ghetto knows this feeling very well. For, above all else, probably the most stressful part for the police working in the ghetto, is this feeling of being constantly on display. The police officer on the beat in every professional sense of the word is an actor, a player who plays a series of interlocking roles. His daily performances must be like being Daniel in the lion's den, before a live audience made up of lions. Clearly the lions are the masters, and the cop must react to their impulse. Or, to put it differently, the ghetto cop is a man on a tightrope before a circus crowd that not only wants him to fall, but urges him to do so for his own good. That same circus performer is also expected to be a lion tamer and clown while he balances himself on that tightrope.

That is one side of the acting. Another is: The ghetto cop has to know how to laugh and cry with his audience. They demand it of him, but such displays of relief, exaltation, or sorrow are tremendously wearing on the nerves when it is almost a daily social exercise. A human being has but so much to give in terms of emotional energy. But there is no limit to what a cop is expected to give in terms of the family disputes, the accidents, the muggings, the murders, the found lost children. He has to share the pain and joy of his clients.

As an actor, the ghetto cop is as much a performer for himself as for his audience. He must constantly remind himself that to fail in the performance of his duty could be fatal. But at the same time he must be relaxed, be the cool cop; for the best performances are given when one is relaxed. Yet, how can he relax when the call coming in from radio central says "There is a man in a bar with a gun."

Then, there are those endless, nervous hours of riding around in a patrol car, waiting to come on stage, watching the night turn into day and the day into night—the house lights go up, the house lights go down. The cop watches the streets, once crowded, become silent, and then he is hit with the feeling of being left out there on his own while others sleep, make love, be with their families. And even when the nervous hours are broken by a job, the cop cannot help but feel that he is a pariah, being shifted from domicile to domicile.

Sometimes the streets are filled with people to the point of overflowing, but they are not people for him to know and become personal with. Any one of them might be his next collar, that person with a gun. They are all suspects because they are black. However, the ghetto cop knows that when his audience looks back at him, he too is a suspect, and he must tell himself, to "be cool, be cool." But, of course, the policeman is a suspect who has been given the right of legitimated deviancy. He has the right to carry a club and gun, two lethal weapons, and he has the right to use them. He has an obligation to use physical force when he deems it necessary. In the final analysis, he must act through a personal interpretation of his role.

Being a ghetto cop is not something that you really can get better at in the aesthetic, rewarding sense. One can only become cooler, more calculating, and efficient in the performance of one's duties. This attitude is greatly encouraged today by the fact that the cop knows he will be required to explain his actions to his superiors. Encouraged programs of police-community relations have been an active, political tool for a number of years now, since the asphalt cowboys were allowed to run roughshod over the black community. It makes the cop in the ghetto believe that when he acts, the uncertainty of his means must be justified by their ends.

The choice of means for the ghettoized cop will become more and more routine—that is to say, the actor in this case has learned his part well. At the same time, the cop can come to sense the alienation of having less to hold onto inside of himself. As a consequence, he tends to react to situations from experience; the cop becomes very visceral in the performance of his duties.

When talking about their present objective circumstances, the police can sound as though they are trapped, persecuted individuals. They can sound as though they are suffering from paranoia, both in the delusions of grandeur and persecution sense. This is true of policemen in general, but more obvious with policemen who work in the ghetto. Paranoia is often attributed to blacks in the context of their being overly sensitive about their objective circumstances in a white social world. However, blacks' sense of persecution is not a delusion. It is real.

Paranoia is a hyper-delusionary state. The ghettoized cop is likely to suffer with his malady which can easily trigger visceral reactions. This is important to the role of the policemen in the ghetto because visceral actions go along with shows of force and violent supervision. The threat of force and the use of force is important for society's supervision of the ghetto. Having hair-triggered attendants for the ghetto institution serves society very well. They can be expected to go off the handle every now and then and commit a violent act, seemingly without any rhyme or reason. The result is that it frightens the hell out of ghetto residents in seeing how vicious police can be without any, or with very little, provocation.

Over the last decade in New York City, practically every year a white police officer is accused of shooting a young, black male, frequently under the age of sixteen, for seemingly no reason whatsoever. There were Clifford Glover, Claude Reese, Jr., Randolph Evans, and John Brabham, to mention some of the names. In a few of these cases, the policeman involved was indicted and eventually forced out of the police department. But most of these incidents were judged to be justifiable cases of homicide. The black community's response to these incidents has tended to be one of fear, forlornness, dismay, and anger.

Psychiatric practice has found that schizophrenia is frequently associated with paranoia. The cop in the ghetto, in very practical terms, is required to develop a schizoid personality as a result of the overall role he has to play. And to be sure, this personality function is nurtured in the police officers by the society overall. On the one hand, people withdraw from the police because of the social role they play; yet people feel drawn to them, because crime is institutionalized in our society. The schizoid nature is also nurtured by the policeman himself who, for example, as a marginal man, feels drawn to the middle class and the mainstream of society, but because his life may depend upon it, also feels compelled to adopt the behavior of the people in the ghetto where he works.

But more than anything, the policeman in the ghetto is likely to develop a schizoid personality, as might many of us who play out job and professional roles in society, because roles by definition are false.

But when you are struggling in a situation of life and death you may well come to take the role as being real, perhaps even more real than the self that is playing the role. This is, indeed, the ultimate commentary on the ghettoized mind.

CHAPTER 5

POLICE ROLES

BLACK ACTORS

In the previous chapter the role and/or roles of the police in the ghetto were discussed. While it was not said, the perspective was specifically from the point of view of white police officers serving in the ghetto. But, we must not forget that black police officers serve in the ghetto as well. Indeed, at one point in the sixties, blacks campaigned very strongly for more black police in the ghetto, feeling that black police officers would be more understanding, more tolerant, more considerate of the black people's plight in the urban ghetto. However, there was a bit of incongruity and implausibility to this argument because it was well known that black police officers, over the years, have been harder on blacks, or just as hard on blacks, as white police officers.

For years, when there were very few black police officers on the force invariably the few were assigned to black neighborhoods. And because the black officers had to fight for acceptance by white officers, they tended to work very hard at trying to separate themselves from black people in general who were seen by white officers as the most criminal, sociopathic element of the society. To demonstrate that they showed no favoritism for this sociopathic element, black police officers would willingly "beat the heads" of blacks, in the name of maintaining law and order. Chester Himes in a series of books created two such stereotypical black cops called Coffin Ed and Gravedigger Jones, who worked the beat in Harlem.

Of course, the demand for more black policemen in the ghetto petered out as our society moved into the seventies. And it was just as well because black officers may be somewhat more sympathetic to black citizens, but because of the required police role in the ghetto they are susceptible

110

to the same forces as white officers. This is to say that the roles we described for white officers in the ghetto are also the roles played by black officers. The difference is not in the roles, but rather in the performance. In this chapter, we will discuss the black officers' performance in the ghetto.

PARIAHS

The pariah character of the police allows them to come to the ghetto with authority and legitimation; yet individual police officers can still be seen as having no autonomous power of their own. This characterization is suited even more so to the black police officers of the ghetto beat. As a South Bronx resident shouted at a police officer in my presence once, "Yeah, you may have that blue uniform on, but it can't cover your black ass. You're still nothing but a nigger, even if you live up there in Scarsdale."

That is the essential point. A black officer is seen as having no authority, no legitimation by virtue of his blackness As a black person he is at the bottom of the social scale as a matter of tradition. The American consciousness has been shaped to perceive black people as being powerless no matter what uniform they put on. If a black man comes to the ghetto as a rule enforcer, then he must come as a tool of the white establishment, for there is no reason for him to come on his own. Therefore, as part of his role, the black police officer is the recipient of much hate from ghetto residents because he appears to be nothing more than the "massa's man," the house nigger who has been sent to the fields to do reconnaissance, the black overseer with the massa's whip.

While there is general animosity for all police in the ghetto, the black officer is the recipient of his own special brand of hostility. The black officer will inevitably be seen, in the final analysis, as an individual who is "a turncoat and a lacky," one who has foresaken his people. The black police officer stands as a mockery to any sense of ingroupness the people in the ghetto might have. And indeed, the people of the ghetto are not wrong in perceiving the black officer in this manner. The black officer, when with his white fellow officers, will speak of ghetto residents as "those people." To ingratiate themselves with white colleagues, ghetto people become strangers to black officers.

For the ghetto residents, the very image of a black person in police officer blue is a factor that weakens their sense of solidarity. Not only has the black officer left the group, but he has turned on the group and become an oppressor. It is very demoralizing and humiliating for ghetto residents to have to accept this. The imperialistic colonizers knew this very well. Once they had conquered a land they would move rapidly to set up a corps of homegrown petty administrators and police constabulary to do their dirty work. It was part of a system of establishing dominance through demoralization. Further, to have a homegrown frontline makes the dominant society appear even more exclusive and paternalism and control can more easily follow. So much hatred can be generated towards black cops by black ghetto residents that white cops can at times, perhaps fleetingly so, be seen as more acceptable by comparison.

Inadvertently then, black cops seem to be a kind of superficial shield for white cops in the ghetto. This is to say that white cops are just a little bit more secure because ghetto residents are more willing, in the first instance, to marshall their free-floating aggression against the turncoats before they push it on the more obvious oppressors.

The black officer of the ghetto is definitely a pariah. First, he is not fully accepted by the white officers he works with, nor is he likely to be accepted or treated equally by the department or the public he serves. He may have the income of middle-class whites, but he would not be accepted into middle-class white communities, and he is likely to be a runaway from a throwaway neighborhood. Nathan Glazer points out that blacks living under our domestic colonial system accrue, by its nature, a pariah status.[1] The black officers who work in the ghetto emphasize this fact for themselves and the people they serve.

Pariahs are made to feel used and abused, and to that degree have no stake in the larger society. When a black person returns to the ghetto as a turncoat and a lacky, these feelings seem to be clearly substantiated. The black officer has escaped living in the ghetto, but the person has become nothing more than an establishment tool. It can make a person feel, "What the hell's the use of trying?" That is, trying to get out of the ghetto and into the mainstream. You are still going to be taken advantage of, even if you put on one of those respected blue uniforms.

But more important, if a person feels that he has no stake in the society that rules his life, that indeed treats him like a social dog, then to be sure he is not likely to care about that society. He is not likely to want to abide by its social rules and regulations and emphatically he is likely to react very strongly when asked to conform. Contrary to the beliefs of the sixties that black officers could be a cooling force in the ghetto, they may very well be, even today, a force that heats up the ghetto.

Paul Chevigny, who did a study of police brutality in New York in the volatile 1960s, made the observation that police, in effect, find it very necessary to force civilians to submit to their authority whenever a contest develops between the two.[2] If the civilian gives way to the demand of the cop for submission, the matter can usually end right there. But if the civilian fails to do so, it can lead to a fracas between the police and the person. Chevigny says this is the basis for police brutality.

Chevigny goes on to say that the people who are most likely to be subjected to a police demand for submission are the minority people, ghetto residents. However, whereas it is easy for affluent people, white people, to say, "I am sorry officer," in response to the policeman's question of, "So you're a wise guy, eh?" That "sorry officer" can be very galling to blacks because such a statement seems to be just another act of submission to the "massa."

It is the job of the police in the ghetto to force the black community to submit to the authority of far removed forces, to unseen forces, to long standing traditions that oppress them. The pariah status of the police makes them more perceivably effective in this role because they are seen more as instruments than as persons. This galling aspect between the police and the ghetto makes it a normal source of tension. Moreover, the black police officer automatically enflames this situation because it is even more difficult for ghetto residents to say they are sorry to the police officer who is black, someone who is perceived as no better off than themselves.

There is a strong mystique to the policeman's uniform that stands in strong support of the police role in the ghetto. The blue uniform seems to encapsulate white officers and strengthens their appearance and thereby seems to strengthen their authority. It makes them contrast sharply with the dark faces around them. It helps to enhance their differences, and therefore gives reason for the right of the white police officer to act differently, if not superior, to the residents of the community. The uniform is also a symbol of the police's pariah status. In fact, as we have said, the mystique is a function of that status. Certainly, it is the mystique which supports the pariah status and the status which supports the mystique.

The black police officer in the ghetto needs all the help he can get to perform the role required of him. But the blue uniform tends not to encapsulate him with the embellishments of strength and authority. If anything, the blue of the uniform flattens and deadens the black officer's appearance. It makes him blend in even more with the people around him. It offers no mystique for the black officer, but instead it helps to remove the symbolic mystique that the uniform normally has. The black officer is not seen as a rule enforcer. He is seen only as a pretender to the throne.

To state the case mentioned above more simply, the following could be said. The blue uniform tends to be a kind of hot medium for white officers because in the eyes of the ghetto residents it heightens and enflames their authority image. But by the same token, the uniform tends to be a kind of cold medium for black officers because it deflates and extinguishes their authority image.

The black officer in the ghetto harbors definite feelings of being the man in the middle, and as a pariah he feels both put down and elevated by the status. Also, this ambivalence seems to be partly responsible for the officer developing a strong sense of mission and purpose in what he does. To be sure, for the black officer there is something desperate in his need to have a reason for doing what he does that goes far beyond any normal sense of duty. This is to say that the black officer, among other things, tends to be more imbued with the Protestant work ethic than his white colleague. E. Franklin Frazier found this a common response of blacks who harbored middle-class values. In our society it is a bourgeois tendency.[3]

Black officers, as a matter of justifying the work that they do, are very willing to see themselves as preventing the criminal and deviant element from taking over the society. They are staunch soldiers in the thin blue line. But at the same time they purposely obscure the fact that the society they want to protect oppresses them. However, the people of the ghetto are not willing to let them forget this. The community is a constant reminder of this, and it makes the officers feel like what they really are, tools and perhaps fools.

It is no wonder then that the black police officer tends to be the most rabid among his colleagues in condemning the ghetto residents for the way they live, for their lazy, sloughly attitude, for their welfare mentality, for the deviants they are. But in thinking this way, he is also condemning himself, for they are seen as he, as being the same socially in the final analysis. This stereotyping of ghetto residents is precisely the way a pariah personality is likely to be described.

The black police officer does not keep these attitudes to himself, but he expresses them to his white colleagues or at least agrees with them when they present the stereotype. This confirms the beliefs of the white officers because they say to themselves if the black cop, who is foremost a black person himself, agrees with the stereotype then there must be substance and truth to it. This strengthens the white officers' rule enforcer attitudes. At the same time, black officers hear from white officers what they want, a bourgeois descriptive put-down of the people they want to separate themselves from. For black and white officers, it all serves as pressure on them to punish the people of the ghetto as a means of confirming their beliefs in the stereotype they want to maintain.

Over the years, the black officers have been known to be very punitive toward other blacks with the least provocation. Since the sixties, their overt actions, as is true of the police in general, have toned down. But given the right circumstances, they can still come down hard on fellow blacks. Yaphet Kiotto, who played a black policeman in the motion picture *Report To the Commissioner* gave a very good portrayal of the black officer who feels he must be punitive towards blacks in the face of whites to justify being a cop.

Black policemen, wherever they might work, are people who go about their duties feeling like men wronged. They frequently discuss among themselves the devious and underhandedness of white officers, their commanders in undercutting their ability to do a good job. As protectors of society, members of the thin blue line, fighting off anarchy, they feel they should be respected, but no, they are scorned. In the ghetto that scorn comes directly from other blacks, and it makes them want to hit back. White officers can play on this reaction in black officers by telling them that if the ghetto residents were like them, law abiding citizens, nonwelfare, not on the dole citizens, then they would not have to be patrolling the ghetto streets. Of course, this is a play on the "you are an example of your race" theme. The black officers are made to feel better than other blacks, while at the same time, they actually are made to feel the same, and as a result this dichotomy triggers automatic vengeance in the black officer toward black residents of the ghetto community.

All of the general problems of pariah status are exaggerated for the black officer; the lust for wealth, the mercenary presence, wanting to desperately win the respect of the community being served.

The description mercenary has the most auspicious meaning for the black officer. He is being seen as a turncoat who is now serving against the community that claims him. Ghetto residents believe that a desire for a steady paycheck is one of the main reasons blacks become cops, and if one talks to black officers they will confirm this belief. However, this can frequently cause black officers, like many white officers, to conclude that, as mercenaries, they should be getting all the wealth they can from their jobs. Yes, for many police officers the bottom line is the money and the bourgeoisie living it can afford. This is an attitude that can produce illicit police behavior. The ghetto is filled with opportunities to capitalize on this. The ghetto can become a place to make a profit from one's position. In this sense the police role as a pariah becomes a business role. And history tells us this has been the route of pariahs in the past.

JUDAS GOATS

The ghetto community is dependent upon the police for essential social services. The police do a job for the ghetto that no other public or private agency does. To this degree the police are accepted in the ghetto, and to that degree they are looked up to. However, few black ghetto residents actually look up to black cops. It is the white cops they minimally look up to. The history of America spells out a relationship of erect whites over deprecatory blacks and this has left deep scars on the black people's consciousness. As a consequence, it is difficult to see the black cop as a person representing a source of power, and therefore someone to be respected, in or out of that blue uniform.

But also, the attitude residents have towards black cops inadvertently lessens any resident's desire to be respectful of white cops. After all, you can lump all those cops together as being individuals of the same stripe, if not the same color. The black officer is then helping to relax a bond of dependency between the ghetto and the white cops. Society would like to see this bond strengthened because it is the blacks of the ghetto who make up the major clientele of the criminal justice system. They fill the jails. They constitute the group that the police concentrates their efforts on. They are the group which society principally wants to isolate, but at the same time control and regulate. A close relationship between the police, the provider of essential services, and the recipient of such services makes it much easier for the police to carry out this task because they become, and appear, less like oppressors and more like Greeks bearing gifts.

Still, the black officer is looked up to by some blacks. He has managed to leave the ghetto and get a job with a steady income. The news media will seek out black cops because they are examples of their race, but also because they are seen as experts on the ghetto. The news media seeks their opinions on the black community, and this forces ghetto residents to pay special attention to these black cops[4] who are put in a position of speaking for the ghetto community. In some ways, the black police officer is pushed to the head of the community by the public and the media. For instance, they are made to seem as good examples for the youths of the ghetto to follow. They frequently become involved in PAL activities. Everyone expects them to because of the clientele being serviced. This is to say that black officers are made more substantively visible than the circumstances might seem to merit when working in the ghetto, taking into account the general societal disregard of the black policeman and his authority.

In the 1960s, when there was a great push to get more black police officers in the black community, the reason most often given for the push was that black cops would be more sympathetic to the plight of black people. While history does not back this up, surely there are black officers who feel deeply about the situation of blacks, and it is likely that they may have become police officers in hopes of being helpful to the black community. But one's own desires are not enough. Take this illustration. Formally, police-community relations programs try to foster positive attitudes in police officers about the black community, which causes some black officers to resent these programs, but at the same time there is an informal mesage that is also being transmitted to the officers.

While police community relations programs have become a loud noise in big city police departments, and it would seem that the police would welcome ways to improve their relations with the black community, matters are still quite desperate between the two groups today. There is a definite, functional reason for this. Antagonisms between the police and the black community help to maintain the adversary status between the two groups which further helps to keep the flow of young black males going into the criminal justice system.

Black police officers, informally, are discouraged from being too helpful or friendly with residents of the ghetto. Such friendliness could hamper the black ghetto cop in his work, his willingness to arrest and so on. In New York City, policemen are not allowed to work in the community where they live for the same reasons already given. More poignantly, however, it is the black cop's colleagues who make it most difficult for him to be genuinely interested in the ghetto community.

Working police officers see the ghetto as a place infected with crime and deviancy. Any police officer who becomes personally involved in that community is thought to have become infected. Black officers are admonished this way: It is suggested to them that close ties with the ghetto probably means that the officer has gone soft on crime. The officer is no longer a dependable member of the thin blue line that is holding back the anarchic hordes. An accusation like this against a black officer can sour his relationships with white officers, and it will make him back off from showing any personal interest in the ghetto community.

This sneaky approach at keeping the black cop away from involvement in the black community appeals to the black cop's feelings of insecurity among his fellow officers. If you want to be accepted, do not be tainted. At the same time, though, the black cop knows that he is expected to be more to the black community than just a rule enforcer. So again he is caught betwixt and between. He can become very sour towards police-community relations programs because he is bothered by the seeming claims that the black community makes upon him. It is the kind of pressure that can make black officers want to quit their jobs, but the financial security is not to be given up. As a consequence, they stew in their animosity and rationalize why they are not taking a more active role in the black community they are serving.

No matter how the black officer is feeling, he is still furthering the pacification of the black community as Commander Bouza talked about it in the previous chapter. This is the case because the black cop falls in line, offering social services, making arrests, doing the police job that the system calls for. But at the same time he is pacifying himself and making life on the job a more marginal one. For he hangs everything on the thin margin of financial existence. This appeals to his mercenary attitudes, but does little, if anything, for his sense of ethnic brotherhood and pride.

Of course, we have pointed out that Commander Bouza refers to the ghetto residents as feral children, and this in effect is labeling them as borderline primitives. By the same token, the white officers can treat black officers as though they are borderline cases. Epithets about black officers are not at all uncommon in police stations in New York City. Frequently, negative comments are made about them on the precinct shithouse walls.

The pressures in the police house and the pressures on the street can make a black officer feel like he is living between two guns. Police officers are required to carry their guns at all times when out in public in New York City. As peace officers, off duty as well as on, they are required to take action if they are aware of wrongdoing. But black officers are squirmish, if not hesitant, about pulling their guns when they are in civilian clothes, especially if they happen to be in the ghetto. If a white man pulls a gun in the ghetto and is holding it on a black person, it is assumed that the man with the gun is a policeman. But that is not the case for a black man holding a gun in the ghetto. Take the following true life illustration:

"I had my gun on them. The one in the middle kept squirming like he wanted to start something, so I told him:

" 'Look, take it easy. I'm scared. You guys just blew two people away around the corner, and, I swear, you start something and I'll kill you—I swear, I'll kill you.' "

"Man, I was really scared," said Police Officer Larry Boatwright as he recalled the incident recently.

He added, however, that after capturing the team of robbery-murder suspects on a teeming street in the Bedford-Stuyvesant section of Brooklyn, he felt an even greater surge of terror when he heard the police sirens cut through the hot, humid, summer night. The police in the radio car—the realization hit him suddenly—would see him, a black man, in civilian clothes, with a gun in his hand on a slum street.

"I was scared they might blow me away," he said, thinking that he might be taken for a criminal.[5]

In New York City, white police officers frequently shoot at, and sometimes kill, fellow officers who are black and suspected of being perpetrators. And usually the only reason for the incident was the fact that the white officer saw a black man with a gun.[6]

Black policemen in the ghetto are to be discredited, to be put down, to be kept in their place. Even in police blue the blacks must appear as incompetent, suspect, and as feral children. The black officers and the community cannot be allowed to form associations, have genuine respect for the other because they might form alliances, and the society does not want that because the black officer is legalized to carry a gun. Historically, when blacks rebelled, it was the black person with the gun who tended to become leader. Our society lives with the mortal fear of the formation of black conspiracies. The late J. Edgar Hoover and the FBI hounded Dr. Martin Luther King, Jr. and the Civil Rights Movement for this same reason. The FBI actually wrote letters to King, telling him that he had to kill himself in order to right the wrongs of his social misrepresentations.[7]

The black cop is a source of social disequilibrium in the ghetto. He has a disorienting affect on residents. They want to trust him because he is black, yet they know if he is a good policeman then he is not to be trusted. He is the worst sort of lacky, turncoat, and Judas. When he put on that uniform, it signaled the fact that he had turned his back on the black community. And the worst part of Judas Iscariot's betrayal was not that he betrayed Christ, but rather that he betrayed his own faith in himself, a faith that rested on the common precepts of right and wrong. The black policeman is in the same frame of mind as the earlier Judas. In accepting gold for his services, he bought off his conscience, but not his soul. Judas's greatest sin was in letting himself be used.

SACRIFICIAL LAMBS

All cops in the ghetto are expendable. If poverty causes deviant and criminal behavior, then more police are not needed in the ghetto, more jobs and education are. Police work in the ghetto is a holding action and nothing more. Their bodies are the sandbags that are used to hold back the unwanted tide. That some of them must die in this effort are the fortunes of war. But as members of the thin blue line, they can reap the glory—an inspector's funeral!

Prior to the 1960s, there were very few black police officers, relative to their numbers in the population, in police departments around the country. It was left to white officers to hold back the ghetto tide and make the required, ultimate sacrifice when necessary. However, the holding action seemed secure enough. The crime statistics had not yet exploded. Then came the sixties and all hell broke loose in the ghetto. The old holding mechanisms were not working well. New mechanisms had to be found and put into place. A new ideology had become the guiding force for the ghetto holding action, the ideology of criminal justice.

The new mechanisms called for the inclusion of more blacks in the police departments around the country. Indeed, through LEAA much of the money for the induction of many blacks into the blue uniforms was federal money. On the tails of police-community relations sermons, blacks were brought in to smooth out, on the surface, the relationships between white police departments and ghetto communities. Suddenly, there were upper level positions for old-time blacks who had slogged through the system for years with little or no recognition. Now they were needed to run community relations offices.

More blacks were being used in the holding action and the new ideology was giving the reasons for their inclusion. Blacks were not to be the catching crooks type of policemen in the traditional American sense of the rugged individualist and the sheriff. They were being included to be community relations personnel. They were being used to make police officers more acceptable in the black community. And while the blacks were being recruited and used for this task, the white cops were playing the asphalt cowboys, putting down the ghetto activism in the most vigilant of manners. And yes, the most mercenary of black police officers were being used as undercover agents in the ghetto to infiltrate the Panthers, the Muslims, and other groups that were trying to push off the yoke of oppression. Black cops died doing this job, sacrificed to black efforts to gain a better life.

It is not long after a black civilian becomes a cop that he realizes that the experience for him is something different. For instance, why is it that his white buddies avoid him off duty? Why is it that white people stare at him so strangely when he is in uniform? Why is it that the black community condemns him as a pig? His white colleagues and the public treat him like a minion. He does not want to admit it, but he comes to see himself as having been co-opted, and he can come to believe that the best way to protect himself is by being a good cop.

Therefore, black cops can become even more rigid about rules and regulations, the laws they must administer, than white policemen. They may try to stop thinking deeply about what they do and this can bring on a rigid rule-book mentality. They will tend to care about the spit and polish of the job. However, these are things that may well be irritants to the residents of the ghetto. Inflexible police can bring on nonsubmitting attitudes. Military type uniforms, soldier-like people sidled with guns, stand out raucously in the ghetto.

The less black cops think about what they do, the better off they are. They appear more comfortable in their work when they perform their tasks by rote. This happens to work very well with the overall task of the police in the ghetto, controlling the people. Indeed, the black cop can become more reliable towards his job than white officers. He will not take off as much time in sick leaves and the like, and when he is on duty he is likely to follow up and respond to all his calls on the radio. And he is likely to spend less time sloughing off in general.

Yes, the black cop may be careful just because he is black and he knows that he is being evaluated by different, likely more rigid standards than white officers. Still the need to perform by rote compliments this feeling and in this way he can be more easily used as a tool against other blacks, and even against legitimate black efforts to gain freedom and equality.

The new criminal justice ideology called for more blacks within the system. The system could learn from black cops, learn about black attitudes that produced the Civil Rights Movement, Bobby Seale, Malcolm X, and other revolutionaries. Also, it is entirely possible that the growth of black studies departments in colleges in the late sixties had as much to do with fighting crime as it had to do with exploring new areas of overlooked knowledge.

For example, LEAA provides a great deal of money for people in the criminal justice system to go to college. Law enforcement personnel take courses in race relations, and even black studies, so they can better understand the black community. A school like John Jay College of Criminal Justice in New York City actually gave black studies courses for police officers in the police precinct station houses. And yes, some black cops became teachers and administrators in colleges, teaching courses to white cops, some of which were about the ghetto.

But, even in a much less formal way, black cops could be pumped for information. As it is, black cops feel obligated to talk about being black to fellow white officers because of the camaraderie among them that acts as a security blanket. Policies of putting a white and black officer together in the ghetto facilitated this transfer of information. Partners tend to become very friendly and outspoken with one another as they go through their tours of duties. A partner can become closer to a cop than to his wife and family.

The TV character Kojak was frequently seen pumping one of his black subordinates about people in the ghetto. In fact, whenever there was a case about the ghetto or black people, the black detective of the series was likely to play a central role in the story. In other words, and to put it more crassly, black cops become, inadvertently, investigative guides to black behavior and the black community. In the same way, black studies teachers are usually black.

Of course, more black policemen on the force did make it easier for the politicians to set up civilian review boards. Since the boards were generally to deal with police brutality, and the brutality was seen as perpetrated primarily against blacks, the boards were usually thought to be a tool of the blacks. But with more blacks on the police force, white officers, or at least their commanders in the first instance, tended not to be so vociferous against the board. Black officers on the force often spoke out for the board, and they had some influence on white officers.

Black officers have come in large numbers in recent years to take their place in a criminal justice system that wanted to change its image from one of coercive control to a system that symbolized, in terms of the black community, one of persuasive control.[8] Black officers particularly in the ghetto have become part of the effort to bring about this change.

Most black officers work in the ghetto not so much because they want to help the black community, but because police departments believe in assigning black officers to work in black neighborhoods. In fact, there is evidence that black police officers would prefer to work in other communities, but because they are black, their assignments are very circumscribed towards the black neighborhoods. They are generally excluded from other precincts as a matter of process and form.

The mere fact that black police officers are more likely to be assigned to ghettos or high crime districts means that they are less likely to put in twenty years and receive a pension. And this is not for the one reason of demise on duty, killed, that is. But the tensions, the stress of working in a high-crime district, of working in a racially segregated neighborhood, of working with negative minded, racially oriented colleagues, can shorten the police officer's tenure of duty. Even more so, these things can bring on hypertension and high blood pressure, elements that are very common among black people on and off the police force.

Also, incidents of mistaken identity of black cops by white cops occur in the ghetto precincts and not in the white middle-class, or downtown precincts. Working in the ghetto puts a black officer in jeopardy from his own white colleagues. Also, within the ghetto precincts the friction between white and black cops runs high. A black police officer in New York, James I. Alexander, who just also happens to teach criminal justice at Nassau Community College, says that white and black officers often exchange verbal abuse, sometimes throw a few punches, and occasionally stage "Mexican standoffs" with guns drawn on each other as a result of racial tensions within the force.[9] For the black police officer working in the ghetto, sacrifice is the proverbial way of life.

COOL COPS

The black cop, like all cops who work in the ghetto, tries to become emotionally detached from his job. The job is not an end in itself, but just a means to an end—to financial security, a middle-class way of life, a pension check. "I'm not here to help my people, but I'm here [in the ghetto] to do a job." So you keep the emotions, as much as possible, out of your work. You withdraw and become as cool as one possibly can.

We have already pointed out that the blue uniform of the police does not enhance the black officer's image; that is, in the sense of giving him a more authoritative appearance. It flattens his image trajectory. When the black cop also acts withdrawn, reserved, and removed from his job activities, this adds to the flat image. Blue, in and of itself, is a cool color, and black is perceived as being a cold color. Add to this cool behavior and you have an uninspiring, lack of confidence image.

The black, cool cop comes off as being one-dimensional, a person without personality substance, without a genuine place in time and space. The image is one of vacuousness. It is the image, in its nice sense, of a benign presentation of self. This has a number of ramifications. For the residents of the community, there is a sense of wanting to reject the cop because there is nothing there of substance to relate to. And this is apart from all the other reasons ghetto residents have for rejecting policemen in general. This could mean, for example, that efforts by black policemen to serve as community relations liaisons are doomed to fail, or be another source of irritation between police and community.

When the black cop puts on his uniform he is giving up his right, if not by intent by outcome, of having control over his life when he is playing out his police role in the ghetto. The uniform extinguishes the person and reinforces the role. Erving Goffman claims this is a serious breach of social existence.[10] And it bespeaks of the black as an invisible man as described by Ralph Ellison, and mentioned earlier in this book.

Now the ghetto residents, of course, do not know what is going on inside of the brain of the black cop, but they can relate to him being cold and uncaring for the people in the ghetto. Now that he has a middle-class income, he has acquired middle-class attitudes.

The black middle class, as a rule, avoids the ghetto as much as possible, but the black cop is an example of that breed that does visit the ghetto. He comes in official capacity, but he comes nevertheless. And he presents an image of the breed that ghetto residents are told they should aspire to.

The image that is spelled out is that of a person who is cold, uncaring, and without feeling for life. But if there is one thing the ghetto residents do have is a feeling for life. It may come from rejection, pain, and hurt, but it is feeling all the same. The black cop comes off as being a person without soul. Soul is a term that blacks use to describe their emotional feeling for life, that part of them that cannot be snuffed out by joblessness, bad housing, and bad education. But this flat personality of the black policeman would suggest that in order to win a place in the world beyond the ghetto, one may have to give up this quality.

Blacks in the ghetto do not want to give up their soul, but that is exactly what the black cops seem to be telling them to do. Give up that soul and you can join the mainstream. Give up that soul and you will no longer be the chief resource of the criminal justice system. Give up your soul and you might be able to cure yourself of the disease of nonwhiteness.

The black cop in playing cool is presenting a highly rationalized state of behavior that is juxtaposed to the highly emotional behavior of the people who live in the ghetto. This may match very well with the increasing bureaucratic nature of our society, but the intrusion of highly rationalized behavior, as an ongoing fact of ghetto life is likely to be a source of friction to residents. It is the black cop's manner that can be so irritating to residents. The way he categorizes and dismisses them, always treating them like objects to be manipulated.

Certainly, as Max Weber has pointed out, the increasing rationalization of modern life has tended to kill off emotionalism in social action.[11] Yet, the stress and strains of living in the ghetto keeps the lifestyle at a feverish emotional level, and if Weber's analysis is correct, the blacks of the ghetto would be at odds with the formal characteristics of society that have become so highly rationalized. This point is mentioned as an aside, and as a refutation of Merton's and others' belief in the idea that poverty is the primary cause of deviant behavior and crime.

We have said that cool cop behavior will spread among the police in society because, in a manner of speaking, they are operating as bureaucrats. As a result they become more separated from the public being served, and they then fall back on their subculture. The black police have even more of a need to fall back on the subculture, but the culture will not give them the same support. Therefore, black policemen will form their own subcultural groups within police departments. Ethnic groups like the Irish Emerald Society and the Black Police Officers' Guardian

Association of the New York City Police Department, for example, are very common to police departments.

The ethnic organizations, the enclaves within police departments tend to further enhance the utilitarian attitudes of the police. The organizations will take positions to support their enclaves over individuals and other officer groups—like special consideration for Jewish cops on the Jewish high holy days and special consideration for black cops on Black Solidarity Day or Martin Luther King Jr.'s birthday, or whatever. Of course, this is all done informally without specific command and administrative okay. The more wedded the black officer becomes to his ethnic organization, the more wedded he is likely to become to a cool cop behavior.

GHETTOIZED COPS

In some ways, it seems ludicrous to speak of a black cop as a ghettoized cop, since ghettoized is thought to mean feelings of rejection, abuse, exploitation, and so on. These elements are basic to the consciousness of all blacks in America. Nevertheless, to speak of the black police officer is not the same as speaking of the black person in general throughout America. There are two very important differences. First, the black cop is not one who is striving for the middle-class lifestyle as much as other blacks because he has it in money terms, at least, and second, he is not one who is likely to live in the ghetto.

The black cop returns to work in the ghetto as a sanitized person. Superficially he symbolizes the black who has been accepted by white society, and given the great opportunity to live the white middle-class lifestyle. He is somewhat made to feel as part of the cream of the black crop, an example to be followed by other blacks. He is made to feel like he is better, and that is necessary if he is to attempt to be a good policeman in the traditionally accepted sense.

For practical purposes, the black cop tries desperately not to see himself as black, and to the degree that he can do this with the help of his tunnel vision, he can be a nonperson in the performance of his ghetto police duties. Therefore, if anything, the black cop is made to feel like a recapture, a person who was ghettoized, freed, but now returned to the ghetto mentality of restriction once again.

To strive for the fruits of success, obtain it somewhat, but to have it blemished in the end, can be so frustrating that it brings on the deepest contempt for society and those being served. With certain politicians, and ghetto residents themselves, still calling for additional black policemen in the black community, the black officer can come to see his role in the ghetto as a result of politicians and community conspiring against him, conspiring to return him to the ghetto. Black police tend to have an unusually strong dislike of politicians, which is not an uncommon trait of police officers who often see the politicians as interfering with their jobs.

Black cops will frequently lament among themselves about their lost opportunity because it is expected of them to be returned to the ghetto. That expectation is disturbing to them. They are taken for granted, presumed upon, just as the people who live in the ghetto. They are disrespected by this attitude of the department and the politicians and the public. Ghettoized means to be taken for granted and ill-considered when being considered at all.

As a black in a black community, the black cop can become laden with self-doubt, another personality trait that is consistent with the ghettoized mind. If he bends to the wishes of politicians and community-minded blacks, he can be accused by his white colleagues of being soft on crime, showing, in Commander Bouza's words, "misplaced generosity." And if he does not follow through in this manner then blacks in the community will be sure to enhance the connotation of pig for him. Either way, the black officer will not feel comfortable. It is the horns of a dilemma for him. And surely, one of the strongest dilemmas of the ghettoized mind is trying to decide whether to stick with tradition or to try to break its hold.

That puts the black police officer in the most awkward of positions because the organization of which he is a part has the main job of attempting to maintain tradition. What is more ghettoizing than to be in a position that causes you to capitulate to tradition while at the same time defending and protecting it? To work in the ghetto is to be confronted by the wish on the part of the community, no matter how benign, to break with tradition. Residents see all blacks as having the same wish, even if it is a black policeman. It makes for a confused situation with the cops. He is damned if he does, and damned if he does not.

Blacks are expected to be prisoners in mind and spirit as a result of being black. The ghetto bespeaks, as Kenneth Clark has said, of walls. The ghettoized cop is a self-imprisoner, a person who feels he is undeserving of full participation in the work environment around him. For the black cop, this tends to happen automatically when he puts on his uniform. The uniform is a definite restriction in the ghetto. It identifies him as an alien and makes him feel perhaps too much like the residents he is supposed to oversee.

Feeling the prisoner, but being asked, if not required, to act free is another aspect of the ghettoized mind. All blacks in the ghetto have this nonsense to put up with, but it is unavoidable because America likes to think of itself as a free society, that in order to participate socially in the society, with any degree of permanent success, one is supposed to act free no matter whether they may feel to the contrary. The fact that so many ghetto residents are maintained by welfare and the inebriations of drink and drugs is an image of how ghetto residents' freedom is maintained. So, they go about trying to express freedom when they do not feel it.

Surely the black cop in the ghetto feels this dichotomy. Dichotomous characteristics of life are expressive of ghettoized feelings and attitudes. To be American or not? A compromise, Afro-American? To be a policeman or not? It is totally contradictory to being a black person in America. Something has to give way. Two ambiguous social roles cannot exist in the same time and space.

Therefore, the black person must pretend being a police officer, just as he must, in working in the ghetto, pretend to be black. Any and all police officers in the ghetto are actors on display. For the black cop, the question in part is how to be on display but at the same time remain invisible. Truly the black cop is the actor acting out the role of the marginal man. He not only exists between two cultures, but he feels threatened, squeezed, and crushed by both of them. To be with black people, but to be unable to identify with them is to be deeply obsessed with the feelings of alienation. It is not whether the black cop wants to identify with the blacks of the ghetto, society makes the identification for him.

Alienation is a normal condition in the ghetto, and as a consequence, says R.D. Laing, most personal actions must be destructive.[12] The ghettoized mentality is one of trying to exist normally in an abnormal environment. That is the fate of the black cop, not as a consequence of the ghetto work place, but rather as a result of his objective circumstances.

Psychoanalysis can expose defense mechanisms that are used by individuals, and they can further expose a number of ways in which a person becomes alienated from himself. Such alienating processes are repression, denial, splitting, projection, and introjection. Defense mechanisms, in psychoanalytic terms, are often described as being unconscious; that is, the person himself appears to be unaware that he is doing this to himself. Even when a person does gain sufficient insight to see that splitting, for instance, is taking place, he experiences it as a mechanism, an impersonal process that can be observed but not stopped.

The black cop is an example of this splitting. He becomes a mechanism for himself. He is transformed when he puts on the uniform. The action becomes the focus of his life, more real than whoever he might be without the club and the gun. As he works in the ghetto, he may indirectly encourage ghettoized thinking and attitudes because it allows him greater feelings of alienation, which inadvertently produces splitting.

Alienation as a term seems to encapsulate all the general ideas of the ghettoized mentality, and indeed when you put the attitudes and behaviors of the black officer specifically with those of the ghettoized cop as mentioned in the previous chapter, it seems to coincide with the descriptive categories of alienation.

CHAPTER 6

THE VIEW FROM THE GHETTO

Once again it is time to turn our intellectual view around in order to get another perspective of the police in the ghetto. This is the perspective from the ghetto. Throughout this treatise, we have largely been looking at the relationship between the police and the ghetto in the third person, always once removed. If our discussion had been taking place in a court of law, most of it would be considered hearsay. More direct testimony is needed about the police role in the ghetto from the residents there who have observed it. As we have pointed out before, the ghetto is perhaps the major force in shaping the police role in that community.

James Baldwin who grew up in Harlem, and who was considered spokesman for the black civil rights cause in the 1960s, once wrote that Harlem had not changed very much from his parents' lifetime to his own. "All of Harlem is pervaded by a sense of congestion, rather like the insistent, maddening, claustrophobic pounding in the skull that comes from trying to breathe in a very small room with all the windows shut. Yet, the white man walking through Harlem is not at all likely to find it sinister or more wretched than any other slum."[1] As former Vice President Spiro T. Agnew was quoted as saying, "If you've seen one ghetto, then you've seen them all," or words to that effect. And who best represents the ever present, yet at the same time forever absent white man? The police officer. It is he who is seen as keeping the ghetto the way it is, keeping the ghetto maddening and claustrophobic and socially inert.

Young black youths are condemned at a very early age to live always in the ghetto. Black youths tend to get police records early which lessens their chances for getting jobs and making a livelihood that will carry them out of the ghetto. They are likely to become aware of hard drugs at an early age, and they can become familiar with its availability. Young people are aware of the fact that the police know about the drug dealing that goes on in the ghetto. They know that the police make no real attempt to stop it. This is an encouragement to the ghetto youths to use it. It seems to be sanctioned by the police, at least in part. Black youths can be all washed up in our society by a very early teen-age.

This is also to say that youths must mature at a very early age. The police, in the way that they talk to and handle the ghetto youths, tend to treat them like adults more than like children. This alone can shorten their growing up time. And much too often, black youths are killed by police in New York City. This adult treatment of black youths is also confirmed by recent events in that Governor Hugh Carey of New York has striven mightily to get a crime bill passed in the legislature (spring of 1978) to treat juvenile offenders more as adults. It will be black youths who will be most affected by the new legislation.

Youths who are treated as adults tend to become hard looking, cold and steely-eyed. They may be thirteen, but they are likely to have the eyes and demeanor of a twenty-five year old.[2] Their steely eyes are set to confront those who would deny them their youthfulness. To the police, those steely-eyed stares are a source of irreverence that must be tested. The youths must be made to submit to the authority of the police.

The police will come down on you for just a stare, so you have to know how to deal with it. For instance, before the officer asks to see your I.D., you take it out of your pocket politely and say, "You want to see my I.D.?" Of course, it will bug the cop because he did not get the chance to ask for the I.D., but you are just doing what you can to deal with the situation.[3]

In Los Angeles, dealing with the police means getting to know and understand them well. To know is to anticipate and perhaps avoid disaster of the worst kind. One gets to know that the L.A. city police are in general the least flexible among the local law enforcement contingent. The L.A. county sheriff's department, whose members see themselves as the local elite, try to maintain a certain distance from the public, and are less likely to harass a person unless you seem worthy. The Compton City cops travel one to a car and come on very strong and tough, like leaning four cats at a time up against the wall and shaking them all down. The juvies ride around in unmarked cars and are all over the place just as soon as the sun goes down. They creep up on you, wanting to know what is going on and saying things that can make a person mad. "Say, who you gonna rob tonight?" But you cannot go for that stuff because that is what they want, get you uptight, get you to react. But you have to be cool, just cool in front of the heat.

For ghetto residents, the police symbolize the power of life and death, the power of the police to take the black person's life as a matter of the officer's discretion. Certainly, this attitude is true for young black males in the ghetto. Prior to the black activism of the 1960s, a white cop could practically kill and maim ghetto residents with almost absolute impunity. Indeed, such incidents rarely, if ever, got beyond the police department's own means of investigation and review. The policeman's word always stood up. Today such incidents might go to the district attorney and even reach the courts. But the chances are very good that the officer involved in a suspicious, noncriminal connected killing of a black will still go free, although with strong probable cause, he might lose his job. A job for a life. It was the suspicious killing of Leonard Deadwyler that helped to trigger the Watts riots of 1966.

The Leonard Deadwyler incident was not unusual for the ghetto, in a meeting between the police and a black man. There is a long standing indignity of cops approaching and questioning black people with their fingers on the triggers of their guns. They prepare themselves to use it, and if they do use it can it ever be called accidental? In the ghetto, the police officer may be scared, and therefore his actions may be reduced to a matter of reflexes. Many a black person's life has been held in the balance of a trembling finger of a police officer in the ghetto.

In the Deadwyler case, the white police officer involved said the shooting of the young black man was an accident. The young man's car moved, causing the revolver to fire, but why was the gun drawn in the first place?

Blacks see their community as overrun with police, "wall-to-wall cops" is what they used to say about Harlem before the city budget crunch caused a cutback in the police force in 1975. And not only do the people of the ghetto see themselves as being overpoliced, but they see their neighborhood as being infiltrated by a special brand of police. There are the tactical patrol squads whose special job is to roam the streets, frequently, if not only, in civilian clothes for the sole purpose of suppressing, harrying and arresting blacks. This is to say that they are not really interested in preventing crime, but rather they are there in the ghetto to respond to black reactions to white authority, like that of the police themselves.

During the 1960s, these special Harlem police were all described as being over six feet tall, with specialized training in judo and karate (those skills that make it possible to kill a man without the use of weapons when a black man learns them, but when provided to the police called simply "instructions in human relations"). The Tactical Police Force was to put in effect the philosophy of police work in the ghetto by the then Commissioner Michael J. Murphy, which was the *substitution of a show of force for the actual use of force.*

Unfortunately, and all too tragically, the show of force does degenerate into the use of force. Today, as always, the police, as the ghetto residents see it, are all too willing to use force. But why should any black community have to put up with even a show of force? The residents of Harlem do feel like they live in an occupied community with so many police among them, but there has been no war fought in Harlem that was so bloody that a "peace-keeping force" was necessary. Yet, it is true that the police treat residents of the ghetto as though they have little or no rights under the Constitution whenever they decide to ignore such rights. The people of the ghetto feel they have no ultimate protection of their rights under the U.S. Constitution. Ghetto people do not have to be accorded due process of the law unless the police and the criminal justice system want to give it to them.

Despair and exasperation are two deep, abiding feelings in the residents of the ghetto. There is the feeling of being swamped by a tide of wretched experiences that degrade you, that remind you of your manipulated lifestyle. There is the feeling of being pushed along, of being hustled, of being told that you cannot be still, that you cannot relax. You cannot be still because the degradation, the exasperation will cause you to be permanently fixed in the hell hole of the ghetto.

And who is seen as the real pusher in the ghetto? Who is seen as *the man?* It is the cop on the beat. He is there with his gun and nightstick to tell you to keep moving. And when you see the policeman who seems to be pushing you all the time, you want, indeed you feel, you have to push back. He ignores your individuality, and he ignores your humanity. He pushes everyone along like cattle. If you are tired, it makes no difference. Everyone has to keep moving, has to be sapped of their energies. It is all a pressure that makes you want to run or fight, and if you stay and fight you find yourself using the same brutal mechanisms, the needle, the gun, that throw you in the path of the police officer whenever he decides he wants to take into account your behavior.

I'm walking in the street 116th, two in the morning all by myself. As I walk I fear—fear some crazy nigger is behind me, walking faster, faster I cross the street. As I cross I see a bunch of junkies in front of the bar and two lesbians making out in the gloomy tenement slum. As I pass the junkies I see a friend taking the stuff in his arm. I feel like scum. I sneer at the cops who don't care! The preacher who on Sunday is so "yes Lord" and just as high from a bag on Saturday night. I see the pimps on 116th Street and Lenox telling the invader girl to get her blonde filthy ass back to 119th Street and work. She begs him not to make her go. He kicks her. I see her and I spit, and inside I say, "goodbye you filthy whore"!

Later I'm on the bus, I vision this old man who slowly drops on his seat. I asked him "Are you tired sir"? He replies "Yes son, I'm tired. Working and living here all my life, giving all my money to the man. I'm old and half dead now."

The bus runs down 125th Street. I see the stores where the man drains our money, takes it back to his family while we starve. I look up the avenue, I see the slums. I say to myself "I gotta do something. Stay and raise hell, or GET THE HELL OUT of here before I'm trapped just like the rest"![4]

The police represent a thoroughly ambivalent force to the people of the ghetto. They are unwelcomed, but at times quite welcomed. Ghetto residents can even understand, as it has been pointed out, that the individual policeman comes to the ghetto as a requirement of his job and not out of a certain personal preference to be an oppressor. Yes, blacks see their environment as being an agitated, hostile, often dangerous world. That makes them recognize the need for law enforcement. They have no one else but the police to turn to. When there is a fight among the neighbors, residents are not unknown to call the police to put down the fight. And occasionally, a streetcorner hustler of numbers or drugs may call the police to report an enemy to settle a score. So then, there is no strict policy of *noncooperation* between ghetto residents and the police. The fact that there must be cooperation is in itself quite galling to the ghetto residents, because in the final analysis, they do not see the police there to protect them. Indeed, they have the feeling that the police do not give a damn about them. "The police say, 'Let the niggers cut each other up.' They don't care as long as it is not in a white neighborhood. They're just watching out for the stores." [5] That is what many ghetto residents believe.

In the ghetto, young people and adults spend a great deal of time out on the corners and the stoops of their buildings, weather permitting. This is particularly true of unemployed males, the men of the streetcorner society as Elliot Liebow called them. Since the police are patrolling the streets of the ghetto in large numbers, inevitably this means that there must be a great deal of contact between these groups. Perhaps it can be said that the relationship between the police and the ghetto is more determined by the interaction between these groups than any other in the ghetto. Therefore, the attitude of teenagers and corner men towards the police are a chief ambience in shaping the police role.

Street people of the ghetto feel harassed, most often, by the police. There is drinking, gambling, hustling, and roughhousing that goes on all the time. The drinking, gambling, and much of the hustle is illegal in accordance with strict interpretation of the law, but the people involved in these activities tend to see themselves as minding their own business and not causing any harm. But their behavior, for the police, is always a matter of a cop's interpretation and discretion. He can let it be, as he probably does most of the time because it can stir up problems the officer would rather not deal with, or he can become involved. The problem for the street people is that they never know exactly when the officer will choose to become involved, need a vice collar or something like that. It is very unsettling to them.

In effect, for the ghetto residents the police are more often than not seen as a source of trouble in their lives. Many residents can tell you when they were arrested—some time in their lives—usually when they were young. And more often than not, the person will consider the arrest unjustified. There is a great deal of talk about being arrested, the reason for it, the results of it, but more importantly how the person handled himself during the process. It is necessary to tell others how you did not let "the man walk all over you."

This points out, and importantly so, that there is an ongoing debate, discussion, and illustration through story and anecdote of the ways black people resist police authority and domination. The desire to resist is precipitous in such contacts, but the weariness of it is also very evident. Take this account:

I just got out of bed and had breakfast, and then I stood here on the stairs and thought about what I should do next, you know, and I had just decided to go over across the street and see some buddies when this police car came up, and the policeman called me. "Hey boy," he said. So I said, "Yeah." And then he said, "Get into the car." "What for?" I said. "Just get into the car." And then when we got down to the precinct I was booked as a drunk. So I said, "Shi-it, I'm no more drunk than you are." So they had to let me go, and I said I'd bring charges against them. Yeah, I really think I should, you know, but I won't, 'cause, see, if I do that he'll be bugging me every time he sees me, and charging me with one thing or another, and I don't want none of that. Would have been another thing if I had lived in another precinct.[6]

The police automatically produce a defensive reaction in the people in the ghetto. That is to say, when the police are present ghetto residents are ready to "show their ass" with the prerequisite stimulation. At the same time, the police presence provokes nervousness and uneasiness among residents. People find themselves sweating, exaggerating their sense of ease, which is really uneasiness when they are around a policeman. And this kind of tension very often occurs suddenly with the turn of a corner, the entrance into the subway, a passing patrol car. While medical facts may not bear direct reference here, this kind of tension can only add to the rather high rate of hypertension that is found among blacks.

What is most interesting about this is that the presence of the policeman, or the fact that he can evoke such tension, can stay with the residents of the ghetto even when there is no policeman in one's presence, or when one is at home with only the thought of the police presence on one's mind. This then can have the anticipatory effect on residents of making them more ready than ever to be defensive when once again they are in the presence of a police officer. How something like this might fit into Paul Chevigny's scenario on the frequent causes of police brutality which was mentioned in a previous chapter, can only be speculated upon.

With this defensive attitude already in the mind of black residents, any police use of such terms as boy or bunny or nigger is only a confirmation of what was already thought to be the police perception of blacks, and this sets up a pace, a kind of communication from the ghetto resident to the police that is easily escalated into a confrontation, a struggle. The fact that so many police in the ghetto show this attitude of disrespect or put down through demeanor, if not words, further aggravates the defensive feeling.

Of course, policemen feel they are just presenting the proper posture for a community that has a high rate of crime and a high rate of deviancy. It is their way of subtly expressing the presence of the law. But it is also a fact of the ghetto resident's life that establishment people often take their presence for granted, as a foregone conclusion of their existence. In many ways, the superficial meetings of police and residents, as perceived by ghetto persons, is one of being taken for granted in the negative, regardless of whether the person has ever had a genuine run-in with the law. They are suspects in a community of suspects and the residents know this. For example, whenever the police are around a black person is not likely to run. It is well known that the police think that any black running in their presence is probably involved with something illegal, even if it is just running numbers.

The basic connection between blacks and the police is fear. Blacks have a long standing fear of law enforcement personnel. After all, most blacks came from the South after the Civil War where they had experienced the horrors of the Ku Klux Klan, who were allowed to kill and maim with police immunity. More than 2,595 blacks were lynched in the South between the years 1882 and 1959.[7] Not one white person was ever brought to trial for those crimes. When a black person is killed by the police without reason, the legacy of the Southern past is recreated. Police brutality also conjures up those old horrors. It was the Southern police who backed the KKK, often themselves being members of the Klan. To many blacks in the ghetto, the police of the North embody the KKK of the old Southland.

In a sense, the police want to engender this fear. It brings on a respect for law and order. But whose law and order? When the black people do not get the fair treatment they feel they are accorded before the law, it is still Southern justice, Ku Klux Klan justice. It is the brutality of "alley justice" that has been accorded their race for 300 years.[8]

THE GHETTO'S VIEW OF THE PARIAHS

Pariah people have always tended to see themselves as strangers in a strange land. They were perceived as strangers because of their different customs and attitudes. The police are perceived in this way, a way that is fully intended by them. They want to be seen as strangers in the ghetto, and they try very hard to act the part. We tend to be more anxious around strangers, more careful, and less expressive and outgoing. It is the way the police would prefer the residents of the ghetto to act.

The ghetto people respond to all aspects of the police role in the ghetto. In particular, the pariah status of the police officer is an inducement of scorn from the ghetto residents. Or to put it differently, the residents see themselves as better than the police insofar as the police officer is an interloper, an alien in their community. The fact that the policeman is seen as some kind of invader, legitimately or otherwise, also forces upon the residents a certain sense that they have to defend their community.

If we turn this idea around and look at it from another perspective what it means is that ghetto residents may see it as their responsibility to challenge the police, their authority, their presence in the black community. This attitude is just another reason why it is so difficult for black residents to submit to white police when they are demanded to do so in the context spoken of by Paul Chevigny, i.e., the police officer asking, "So you're a wise guy, eh?"

Therefore, when the resident fails to comply with the police officer's demand for submission it is more than just being a smart ass or acting defiant to authority, it is a posture of aggressiveness, of challenge, and of defense.

The police have always been somewhat astounded by the fact that so many blacks are willing to confront them, contest their power, and indeed take them on, in the face of the police officer's weapons, the nightstick, the gun, and other reinforcements to be called upon if necessary. Such individuals who are willing to fight the police with the possibility that they might even be killed if the police officer feels so threatened, are usually classified as crazy niggers. This is precisely the class of black that the Black Panthers were put in and, to a lesser degree, the Black Muslims. Malcolm X with all his talk of the white devils, of whiteness itself being a kind of sin, made it easy for establishmentarians to attack him with the crazy nigger label.

For the cop in the ghetto, the crazy nigger label is, in part, a backlash from his pariah status.

THE GHETTO'S VIEW OF THE JUDAS GOAT

There is no doubt that the police serve a most important role for the ghetto in terms of the social services they perform. Without such services, the ghetto would be a much more downtrodden, volatile place for those who live there. By offering these services, the police bring about certain feelings of ambivalence in residents towards them. It may be a type of love-hate relationship which is furthered, deepened by the police officer's Judas Goat role.

When the ghetto residents deal with the police it is very much like being soothed by the right hand while being choked by the left hand. It is the feeling of being both helped and hurt at the same time. It is also a kind of restraint, generally among ghetto residents in taking actions againt those they may feel are truly their oppressors. The police are seen as being needed for protection against crime and they are also seen as a necessary lynchpin of the community, therefore to attack them is to endanger the well-being of the community.

This kind of ambivalence makes it difficult for the blacks to see the police in a totally negative light, and therefore the riots, for example, were sure to turn out to be more of a positive light for the police and a negative light for the blacks. What the Judas Goat engenders in the life of the ghetto community is a clear, continuous stream of ambivalence that protects the role of the police, but further exposes the people of the community to pacification and control of their general life by the police.

And perhaps the chief perception of the Judas cop's role in the ghetto is that of exposing the residents to their sense of inadequacy, their dependability, their sense of weakness. For this is the way they are made to feel—like the feral flock being led by the nose deeper into the ghetto. And it goes without saying that the police make the ghetto residents feel like children in this capacity. They are called in to solve the people's problems because the people cannot solve them. But it is not only that the people cannot solve their problems, but also that they had to come once again to their betters, their superiors, to straighten out the difficulties of their lives. In the social Darwinist sense, these ghetto blacks are living off the herd instinct that allows them to be led as a feral flock.

THE GHETTO'S VIEW OF THE SACRIFICIAL LAMB

The people of the ghetto know that police die in their community, and as the newspapers will say, the officer died in the line of duty, trying to ensure law and order and protect members of the black community. The crime goes on. Another life was sacrificed. But do the ghetto residents feel sorry about the tragic death of a policeman in their community? It is difficult for residents to feel genuine sorrow for the cop. Why? Not so much because they hated the individual policeman, whom they probably did not know, but rather his sacrifice was seen, more or less, as something that the policeman brought upon himself, and because most cops in the ghetto are perceived as a Dirty Harry or a Kojak, out there in the black community as a hand of the establishment, and as a person playing out his masculine role of the rugged individualist.

Why feel sorry for a dead cop? When he was alive he probably enjoyed his work in the ghetto of oppressing black people. The residents know little about the fact that police officers are appointed to the ghetto, most often without their consent, at least in the first instance. From their point of view, the cops are in the ghetto because they want to mete out alley justice to black people.

One does not cry over the passing of a policeman in the line of duty. One only laments his coming in the first place. If he had not come into the community acting like a thug, then he probably would not have been dealt with like he was one. These are bitter reactions to the tragic end of another human life, particularly in light of John Donne's poem *For Whom the Bell Tolls*. But for others to see the death as a sacrifice, they must be able to relate to it in the personal sense that the individual was doing something for them, perhaps something they could not do for themselves. In this context, the sacrifice is not evident to the ghetto resident. Indeed, it is not that the police, even with their social work activities, are in the main doing something for residents, but it is in the main that they are doing something against them.

THE GHETTO'S VIEW OF COOL COP

The attitudes and behavior of the role of cool cop in the ghetto fits very smoothly with the residents' perception of the police. They relate to a cop not as another human being as much as they relate to him as a thing which is distant and impassioned about the circumstances of the community in which he finds himself. He is to be seen as a machine, there to do a job. To put it differently, what this essentially means is that the residents do not relate to a person in the blue uniform, but they relate to an actor who is playing a role.

Many programs have come forth as a means to better the relations between the police and the ghetto, but these programs make the assumption that the two groups relate to one another as fellow human beings who just happen to have a problem. But the police officer comes to the ghetto with his mind filled with stereotypes. The ghetto residents do not see a person in a blue uniform, they see a minion of the establishment, the oppressor, a pig. They both are playing roles and relating to roles. The ghetto is one big stage that separates actor from audience, and audience from actor. How do you better the relations between the audience and the actor when stage presence demands that there be a separation between the two? You do not! And, the cool cop status enhances and strengthens the separation.

The cool cop is very symbolic of society's cold shoulder to the ghetto, to society's turned off attitude about the throwaway people. The cool cop is what the ghetto residents have come to expect in their police officers. Indeed, a more caring group would really come as a shock. The police role in the ghetto is more of a hidden agenda than it is an open expression of intent. Indeed, cool cop is cool to hide his feelings and emotions, and that is what the actor must do, subordinate his personal feelings to the demands of his role.

THE GHETTO'S VIEW OF THE GHETTOIZED COP

It is almost impossible for the ghetto residents to relate to the police in the ghetto as a rejected, abused, exploited group like themselves. While there is every indication that the cop who works in the ghetto is psychically and socially little better off than most ghetto residents, such a view is almost incomprehensible to ghetto people.

For the ghetto residents, the cop is a paragon of middle-class rewards and lifestyle, a person who represents the establishment in the black community. That he is ghettoized like the black people, that he suffers alienation, a sense of powerlessness, and may think of himself as being an outcast, just does not make much sense to black people. The years of police oppression in the ghetto have opened a wide girth between the police and the residents. But, unfortunately, it is that same girth which binds them together, and stimulates the friction between them.

The people of the ghetto would find it most difficult to relate to cops as being prisoners like themselves in the ghetto. The police have freedom of access throughout society. Ghetto residents do not, to be sure; it is the police who help to prevent ghetto residents from having free access to the rest of society. They guard the exits and entrances to the ghetto. They intimidate residents, telling them to stay in their place and give way to police authority or suffer alley justice.

The ghetto cop may very well laugh and cry with his ghetto audience, but at some point he can stop playing his role and go home to his middle-class community, and this is a grave distinction between the ghettoization of the cop and the ghettoization of those people who live in the ghetto. There is some relief for the cop but there is no relief for the residents, and part of that "no relief" comes from the cop himself. For cops may leave and change shifts, but there are always new shifts, and new cops to keep the pressure on the slum dwellers.

CHAPTER 7

CONCLUSION

We have now surveyed the role(s) of the police in the ghetto, and if nothing else the experience suggests that perhaps we should begin to look at the police presence in our society differently. Yes, the police do catch crooks and they are concerned with law and order, but that is not the primary reason for their presence in the ghetto in such large numbers. Indeed, it could be said that the police presence in society as a whole has little to do, in the first instance, with catching crooks. In trying to understand the role of the police in society, all too frequently we have allowed the description of police functions to become our definition. Unfortunately, this never takes us further than reflecting on the image of the police that the police want us to see.

The presence of police in our society has nothing to do with the *good guys* and *bad guys*. It has more to do with the presence of police in a *policed society*.[1] America is a policed society. This is to say, our society has a professional corps of police officers, stationed throughout civilian communities, who exist for the sole purpose of policing the citizens. They exist as an arm of government, and they have been given the authority and physical potential to exercise violent supervision over the citizenry. Violent supervision has been a fact of black people's lives in America for over 300 years. At the outset, this suggests a basic affinity between our policed society and the ghetto. But to be sure that this relationship is maintained, the ghetto is classified as a community of insitutionalized deviancy.

However, the most significant fact about the police in a policed society is that the policing mechanism is also the same mechanism by which the government, on a day-to-day basis, penetrates the citizens' daily lives. This is the government as it stands for the status quo, traditional American values, and the mainstream of America's central political authority. Edward Shils states that there is a need to have a close integration between the social periphery and the social center of modern, democratic society.[2]

Democratic society is consensual by nature. Therefore, its political, social mechanism must be constantly concerned with any and all aspects of society that would affect the status quo, basic values, and ongoing political ideology. The level of consensus, or at least the appearance of consensus, must be maintained. Therefore, the social periphery must be constantly pulled in towards the social center of society. It is the responsibility of the police, when necessary, to pull the social periphery closer to the social center. So then, it was the police in the 1960s who went about their business of attacking and destroying the Panthers, the Yippies, the hippies, anti-war and student activist movements because they represented values that were straying from the social center.

In this context, of course, the ghetto as a labeled community of institutionalized deviancy appears to society as an adversary. The ghetto interferes with society's striving for consensuality. However, the idea of consensuality in itself is but a rationalization that hides the racism that is mobilized towards the black community. In essence, the police are policing the ghetto because a nonwhite population lives there. This population has been declared unfit to live with their white betters, unfit to participate fully in society, and unfit to be treated with decency and respect. The history of race relations in this country bears this out, and like the early European Jews, the blacks have been enshrined in the ghetto because they are basically seen as a threat to society. The American democracy functions with allowances for keeping blacks segregated in ghettos, separated from the rest of society by a buffer of police authority.

Another point that seems to be clear in the relationship between the police and the ghetto is that since the police must pull the social periphery back to the center of society, they are acting as a conduit for mainstream values that are used to confront ghetto residents. At the same time, the police are being confronted by the values of the people in the ghetto that will tend to run counter to the general values of the mainstream. The police are being influenced by the values of both sides of their social ledger. They bring values into the ghetto, so to speak, and they carry values out of the ghetto. This is significant because the police become carriers of the values they are supposed to extinguish.

Take for example the way the police fought and resisted the demonstrations by civil rights activists in the early sixties. They did so to protect the establishment, and they thought such demonstrations were anti-American. Yet, the police in New York City picked up on the same tactics in the seventies as they fought for increases in salaries. Police fought with police to get their own way. And, the police helped to spread the drug culture because of their own reaction to it. They went out of their way to punish the hippie types which helped to give them greater exposure in the news media and more young people became aware of it as a result. And look at the way the police allowed themselves to be exploited on TV and in motion pictures in terms of their attitudes on drugs. This exposure very likely helped to spread the drug culture rather than hinder it. Young people enjoy rebelling against authority, especially police authority. This is contrary to James Q. Wilson's notion that the black youths in the ghetto helped to spread the epidemic of drugs to middle-class whites who went to help the blacks in the ghetto during the sixties.

ASPHALT COWBOYS

We began this book with the statement that there is confusion in the role of the police in the ghetto. The reason, in part, may be due to the fact that the police officer is not consciously and rationally aware of the true nature of his role in the black community. He likes to think of himself as being in the ghetto to maintain law and order, even when his experiences are telling him something different.

The police officer on the beat is largely unaware of the fact that he is being used in the ghetto as an asphalt cowboy to round up the social strays and to keep the lock on the corral gate. He does not think of himself as a political instrument that is being constantly manipulated to satisfy the whims of this nation's central political authority. In the 1960s, the ghetto was drifting away from the center of the society. There was the call for "Power to the People!" and "Community Control!" This was in a sociopolitical direction that was entirely new to our society. So the police were turned loose to roam the urban range and pick up the strays.

The labeling of a community as one of institutionalized deviancy is a means by which society gives directions to the police in telling them which groups need to be herded back into the fold. This can be seen with homosexuals, prostitutes, and religious groups like Reverend Moon's Unification Church, the Hari Khrishnas and the Jesus freaks. Reverend Moon's followers are "moonies," the new Jesus lovers are just freaks. The ghetto is filled with jung' bunnies, spooks, apes, shines, mau mau. These terms or epithets make it easier or the police to use violent supervisory force if necessary, because they see themselves as not dealing with American citizens in the ghetto, but rather they are dealing with the mau mau, for instance.

In the 1960s, quick action was needed to put down the massive anti-establishment activities that were occurring all across America. A massive police response was needed. A new ideology was required. The academic community was ferreted out to give support to the new response; in part, because teachers do well at promulgating ideologies, and because plutocracy is a very important phenomenon in modern society. We listen to academicians even when they have nothing really new to say. The criminal justice ideology became another possessed subject of academia and thereby it was understood to be legitimate and in good standing.

The academic studies of police, their involvement in community relations programs, which really are addressed to police and ghetto relations, constitute little more than exhorting propaganda that calls for the police to take drastic action to pull the ghetto periphery back to the mainstream before it brings the entire society down upon our heads. Having the blacks so far out from the mainstream is in effect dangerous to the well-being of society as a whole.

The police come to the ghetto as colonialists, ready and able to suppress the natives. From the point of view of the police they come to the ghetto with the consciousness, the social Darwinist attitude that struggle must exist between white and black men, that the "survival of the fittest," as a course of human action must be played out. The ghetto is a proving ground where white can show its superiority over black. Tom Hayden says that it was the police who started the riot in Newark, and it was the police who maintained it. Therefore, the ghetto by sword, gun, club, or words of intimidation, must be captured and subdued time and time again.

SOCIALIZATION

Recruitment to the police force is an operation that supports the covert purposes of the police. Most of the men entering the New York City police force are likely to be from lower-middle-class or working-class backgrounds that encourage a certain ethnocentricity and bias towards blacks. Such a background is known to encourage a physical rather than a verbal method of resolving conflicts. A person of this background on the police force is likely to communicate with the public in an authoritarian and paternalistic manner, and would assume that citizens could not be expected to be compliant without discipline and control.

Recruits come to the police force as borderline failures. It is probably their last chance to have a decent middle-class way of life. To this degree they are status seekers. People who get in the way of their attempt to fulfil their aspirations are going to receive their wrath. The ghetto people are poor, many of them are on welfare. The police see them as being on the dole, cheating society, and ultimately cheating them because they, the police, are on the city payroll too. The police officer is all too ready to punish the ghetto resident for being on the dole and denying him his just due.

Police recruitment seeks out young people with compliant, insecure personalities. Such individuals are likely to be much more sensitive to threats of any kind against society and its general well-being. This also means that such individuals are likely to be more than willing to apply violent supervision to ghetto residents, and the public in general, when the command to do so is given.

People with liberal attitudes, Arthur Niederhoffer pointed out in his book *Behind the Shield,* are likely to be screened out of the recruits who eventually make it onto the New York City police force. As a consequence, more conservative police types are likely to make it on the force, but these types are likely to be more intolerant of the people in the ghetto. And it is a person of this character who is likely to hold more to traditional values, the values of his forefathers, the values of the mainstream.

The police department of a large urban city turns out a great deal of statistics, statistics that are used to justify the worth of the agency. The statistics will cover all points, from times of arrest, conviction, imprisonment or release of the criminal. These statistics tell of the efforts of the police in corralling and returning particular individuals to society in the capacity the system wants to accept them. The society has to be continuously appraised on how the center's values are suffering or being protected and maintained. Numbers of arrests are important to the police department. Numbers of arrests are important to appraising the center's values.

These statistics tend to support the rule-book mentality of many police officers. This is a very negative phenomenon for the ghetto because the problems of the people there are rarely considered when the cop is trying to do his job. They do what they think their commanders want, and not what is best for the people being served.

Remember, the cop on the beat generally does not understand his real role in the ghetto, therefore, it is very important to him to have his commanders back him up, because he believes that they know what the score is. In the same way, the cop believes that to get the desired backing, he must do what he thinks his commanders want. In the 1960s, their commanders wanted them to get rid of the Black Panther threat, so the Panthers were decimated in vigilante style.

Police officers, because of their puritanical background and upbringing, tend to be Calvinist messengers. That is, they believed, for example, that work is good, that work is done for God. Consequently, anyone who does not work is ungodly, and perhaps needs to be punished. Officers bring these Protestant ethic attitudes to the ghetto and punish the residents for being unemployed and on the dole. This is a basic attitude that aggravates the relations between the police and the residents of the ghetto.

The fact that police are borderline losers, persons who tried other jobs and failed, makes them feel very much on the level of blacks in the ghetto. To help keep their distance and security intact while working in the ghetto they may feel that they must show their superiority over the residents; so you have Paul Chevigny's scenario of the police forcing the residents to submit to their authority and will. This scenario works very well for the police when they must use violent force. Using force is to make someone submit to your will.

The nature of the police officers' lifestyle induces them to form a subculture. Rodney Stark says that a police subculture by its nature puts itself at odds with other subcultures, in our society, particularly the black subculture. A police subculture is possessed of its own values, as are other subcultures. Members of a group will be very cognizant of their values because they are a subculture. In the same way they will tend to find other values of other subcultures distasteful. The fact that the ghetto contains black people who society ostracizes makes it even easier to hate the values of that subculture. This can help generate hostility when violent supervision is called for on the part of the police.

THE MEDIATORS

With the police not being aware of their covert mission in the ghetto, the phenomenon of the self-fulfilling prophesy serves them well. According to Robert K. Merton, the phenomenon of the self-fulfilling prophesy allows the person's perceptions, even if they are wrong, to take precedence over reality. So police officers who come to work in the ghetto, will bring their preconceived ideas with them about the ghetto, and they will see only a community of institutional deviancy. They then act out their roles in accordance with their preconceptions. Or, to put it in the words of W. I. Thomas, "If you define a situation as real, it is real in its consequences."

In this context, no matter how brutal a police officer might have to become working in the ghetto he can always rationalize his actions in terms of his law and order functions. To be sure, it will be difficult for him to see his actions in any other way, according to the theories of Merton and Thomas. If such is the case, then the police make a good political tool to have in the ghetto.

The must win reflex is also an indication that the performance of the cop on the beat is beyond his rational mind. But it translates into the "I'm not taking any crap" attitude which can make a simple situation, according to the Chevigny scenario, develop rapidly into a situation of confrontation.

The police as rule enforcers in the ghetto clearly example a force concerned with social values. Rule enforcement is used to justify the policeman's presence. This is to say that enforcing traditional values will be a source of justifying their job. It is easier to do their rule enforcement job when it is believed that it is a mandatory action towards those being served. Police tend to be stuck with the notion that the public is wracked with original sin. It is easy to have such perceptions in the ghetto because black is seen as bad and sinful. It is a good Protestant way to look at the world.

As rule enforcers, the police protect society's basic values. At the same time, in the capacity of social brokers they act out the promulgation of society's norms while being a buffer between the ghetto and the main-stream. In the social broking exercise, subtlety is more the rule in trying to pull the social periphery back to the center. For example, the police work in PAL imbuing the kids with a sense of hard work and fair play, specifically as it relates to the Golden Gloves tournaments. PAL shows that having societal norms makes it easier to negotiate the system. Many a boxing champ has come up from the ghetto through the Golden Gloves.

The capacity of the police as colonial guards in the ghetto serves to demonstrate another side of how they try to pull, or force the periphery of society back to the mainstream. It is the function of the police to prevent the ghetto and its people from developing social, political, and economic coalescences. Groups such as the Black Panthers, the Muslims, the Blackstone Rangers were infiltrated by police informers who worked to destroy the groups' effectiveness, while at the same time they fed the news media discoloring information about the groups. That is why, to this day, most white and black Americans do not know the message the Black Panthers were trying to deliver. By not allowing new values and ideologies to arise in the ghetto, the people are being forced to stay with the old ones even though they may not be serving them well.

The police are guardians of the status quo and to this degree they must protect vested interests which result from America's ranking or stratification system. This is to say that the police are much more likely to be a force for conservatism than liberalism, and given the status of the black ghetto this fact alone puts the police in a contentious situation with those people. Moreover, to do their jobs, the police have to be essentially strati-philes because they are expected to serve the values of the social center. The higher people are in the ranking system, the more they will represent the social center. The lower they are in the ranking system, the less they will represent the social center and the more they will represent the social periphery. Stratiphilism serves the social center.

THE ACTOR AND HIS ROLES

The police officer comes to the ghetto as a pariah, floating flotsam and jetsam in a sea of blackness. They bring no commitment to the community where they work, no affection for the public they will serve. Ghetto residents see them as an outcast group interloping in their community. The police are made to feel unwanted and undesirable. And they there-fore do feel a certain freedom that allows them to be as bizarre, as secretive, as underhanded, as chicanerous as they like to do the work in the ghetto. And too, it was the pariahs who came with their own values, those values that were quite different from the social system they found themselves in. Pariahs think of their values as being more important than other groups', and this fact always caused friction for them among the groups they associated with. In the ghetto that group is the black residents.

The Judas Goat leads the other goats to slaughter. The police, contrary to all the opinions ghetto residents have about them, are in a real sense one group that is a leader in the black community. They lead the residents to the social services they need when most agencies are closed. This may help individual people but it probably hurts the community in the long run because it diffuses social discontent and placates needs while not solving the underlying social problems. Further, the services the police provide also keep the community closely wedded to the police which allows the police to stay deeply involved in the personal lives of the people of the community. They are continuously penetrating the personal lives of the people in the community by offering social services to them.

The cool cop in the ghetto is emotionally detached from his work, striving for efficiency. The cop has become an instrument for bureau-cratic penetration and the proliferation of bureaucratic values; which is to say, spreading such values as they are representative of the social mainstream.

THE VIEW FROM THE GHETTO

The police come to the black ghetto as a force that is to be used specifically to dominate the lives of the residents there. Whatever else they might do, that fact is essential to the role they perform. They may offer the residents social services, involve the young people in PAL, and conduct writing contests with the winner becoming police commissioner for a day. But, in the end, what the people of the ghetto will feel is that they are being dominated and controlled. There is no way to respect the police as individuals if you feel that what they want to do in the end is dominate you. Yes, you can show a healthy regard for their ability to dominate you, with gun, club, and the legitimacy of their authority, but this is not an attitude that produces respect.

At the same time, a closeness remains between the police and the people who live in the ghetto. There is a recognizable dependency that exists between them. Young black males from the urban ghetto are the chief resource of the criminal justice system. In a real sense, there would be no justice system or police as we know them without the young black males who are forcibly taken into the system by the police. As all agencies and systems want to further their lives, the flow of the major resource for the system must be maintained. The closer the system can be to this major resource, the better it can control the continuous flow of bodies that are needed into the criminal justice system as a whole.

Of course, looking at this matter from the perspective of the police having the responsibility of pulling the social periphery back to the established center, there is justification for pulling blacks into the criminal justice system. The black subculture does fall outside of the mainstream, and the strays must be continuously rounded up.

Yes, the people of the ghetto feel that white society is using them, or better still, exploiting them for social, physical, and psychic reasons. Looking from the ghetto is like looking out of a pen, and the police are attendants. They can take you out of the pen or they can force you back into it. They can enter the pen whenever they want to, and leave whenever they choose, but the ghetto resident finds himself a prisoner there. The ghetto resident sees himself as having no rights except those which his attendants will allow him to have, and that is the clearest statement that can be made about the police role in the ghetto.

THE PERPETRATOR

Some readers, undoubtedly, will conclude that this book is essentially an attack on the "honky police." "The guy has an ax to grind." However, such a surface conclusion would certainly miss the point. While it is true that the police have been singled out as an interstitial focus for analysis, this treatise has repeatedly stated the case that the police are but a cog in a much larger wheel. As goes the wheel, so go the police.

At the same time, I am aware of the fact that surface conclusions do have their appeal. As has been shown, social scientists who study police-community relations stress the problems of the ghetto that inhibit law enforcement, but the influence of society as a whole in the relationship tends to be minimized. Yet, we know that the police as a group are not self-creating. They are a product of our social system. It is not the police, in and of themselves, that socially overall maintain the ghetto as an institution. Moreover, it is not the police role, in itself, that determines that the police will function as institutional attendants in the ghetto. The police, like the people of the ghetto, are locked into a social constellation that predicts, if not requires, a certain behavior from them. When a police officer puts on his uniform and works in the ghetto for all practical purposes he becomes a part of an institution that society has designated for throwaway minorities. His behavior is a consequence of this fact.

Consistant with the surface appeal, the role played by the police in the ghetto, and the reaction of the residents to it, is emphasized as *the* major problem in police-community relations studies. But more accurately, it is the role of the police in society that is *the* problem, and as Jerome Skolnick pointed out more than a decade ago, *that problem* needs to be under closer scrutiny.

What can be done about the situation of the police in the ghetto? To begin with, since the problem goes far beyond the police themselves, the police obviously cannot change it as a fact of their own consciousness and/or merit. The roots that shape the situation go deep into our social structure and culture, and unless change occurs at this level, it is not likely that the situation of the police in the ghetto will alter much for the better. Specifically, as long as the label of being *nonwhite* is perceived in this society as a prognosis of a social disease, then the police will be used to oppress those people who have been so labeled.

However, perhaps there are some things that can be done to at least lessen some of the friction that exists between the police and ghetto residents. The following are only modest proposals because trying to cure symptoms tends to distort the true nature of innate problems. Nevertheless, I would make these suggestions.

It would be helpful to the situation of the police in the ghetto if the police were made aware of the actual social roles(s) they play in that community. If they are institutional attendants, they should be so informed. Let them know that they are more guards than guardians, and that behind prison walls guards can become prisoners too. Maybe such an awareness will make the police more empathetic to the plight of ghetto residents.

By the same token, if the police are colonial guards, they should know this because it would tell them a great deal about how society actually sees them in their role in the ghetto. For instance, individual colonial guards have always been expendable, destined to commit altruistic suicide to protect socially endowed vested interest. Might not the police think differently of themselves if they realized that, in the final analysis, they are being used as mercenaries?

The role the police are being asked to play in the ghetto is dehumanizing, causing a disrespect for others and themselves. With the police being one of the most important groups in our social system, society loses the most because of this. In this sense, the police, as the thin blue line, may not be holding society together, but helping to tear it apart. Police need training in ethics and morals, because in the final analysis the treatment by society of the people in the ghetto is immoral. Immoral behavior by officers is one of the biggest problems for the police in the ghetto.

Because the police are a pariah group in the black community, they feel little social and personal kinship with the people. There is a vacuum between the two groups which encourages mistrust, misunderstanding, adversity, and fear. Perhaps the police should, as is the case in some other countries, be required to live in the community where they work. Yes, there would be a great deal of police, if not public, resistance to this because our society is based upon separate, racial, ethnic, and socio-economic communities. Still, such a move could be a big step towards breaking down this pattern of segregation, and it would be an indication that a major force in society was willing to recognize the fact that being *nonwhite* was not a social disease.

But most important, organizational change is needed in the police bureaucratic structure. The change that I would recommend would also back up the idea of police officers living in the same community where they worked. The change is this: There should be a measure of community control over community police. There should be local, community police boards with the power to hire and fire police officers and their commanders, or otherwise prevent them, legally, from working in their community. There would still be a central police authority, the department, which would do the basic screening of candidates and train them, maintain the salary structure, pension funds, and so on, and generally coordinate the police function within the criminal justice process as a whole. The local boards would not make law, or usurp the policymaking functions of the central police authority, but what they would have is the *right of review*, with the power of rejection, over qualifications and behavior of an officer who wants to serve, or wants to continue to serve, in that local community.

One of the main objectives of this type of approach would be to reduce this notion that police work for the amorphous entity called society. Much is done against the people of the ghetto in the name of society. But under this suggested organizational aegis, the police would not, in the first instance, work for society, but rather they would work for the community where they serve. It would be the people in the community who would determine if they are performing their duties in accordance with the *rule of law*.

An organizational set up like this for the police is not without precedence. New York City already has local school boards that function somewhat in this fashion, and the early American frontier had sheriffs who owed their jobs to the communities they directly served. This last suggestion is also in keeping with the idea that the police are supposed to serve the public, and not that the public is in service to the police and their functions.

These are only a few suggestions that might ease some of the tensions between cops and ghetto residents, but in no way would they bring about the fundamental changes in our society that are needed to solve the police problems of the ghetto. Racism is a moral problem for this society, and America has shown that it is unwilling or unable to confront this issue on moral grounds. Therefore, indignities towards nonwhites begets indignities, and repression begets repression. There is no final end in sight.

BIBLIOGRAPHIC COMMENT

The writing of this book was inspired principally by two works, Jerome H. Skolnick's *Justice Without Trial* and Michael Harrington's *The Other America* (and of course my own personal experience). Skolnick studied the police during the explosive years of the 1960s, and he points out that while the police would have us believe that the *rule of law* is their primary objective, their actions are greatly flawed by the quality of their work, particularly as it relates to certain groups in society.

Michael Harrington's essay on the forgotten Americans during a time of general affluence shocked America into rediscovering the poor at the beginning of the 1960s. In trying to describe the plight of that other America, he remarked that what was needed was "an American Dickens" to fully record the quality of life of the poor in this society. I have tried to remember that statement as I wrote this book. More than sociological jargon is needed to describe the police role in the ghetto.

James Q. Wilson is recognized as an authority on police behavior and crime in America. His books *Varieties of Police Behavior* and *Thinking about Crime* are works that were helpful to the analysis in *The Police and the Ghetto*, even though I strongly disagree with many of the ideas he seems to have on crime and how the police and society can, and should, deal with it.

Arthur Niederhoffer's book, *Behind the Shield*, is one that free associates on the police experience. It is important because it shows the continuum of police experience from neophyte to seasoned veteran. The fact that the author himself was a New York City policeman for more than twenty years clearly comes through the exposition by the weight of its insight.

Rodney Stark's *Police Riots* is an extremely valuable work. Stark takes the position right out front that the police as a force in society are a problem, and a very dangerous one at that. The police have established a motif of a routine use of violence, and it has been established as a fact of their normal duties and responsibilities. This police violence erupted into police riots in the sixties as a fact of routine police procedures. The ghetto residents easily fell into this police violence mosaic.

Samuel Yette's *The Choice* is a searing indictment of American society's cold, vicious efforts towards black genocide. According to Yette, the blacks are in a struggle for survival as a citizen group in America. Advisors in the White House, during the sixties, urged the internment of black youths, and sterilization programs are being used to prevent black births. And at street level, the police have been given the go ahead to stop blacks from coalescing as a civil rights, political, or paramilitary force. Yette's thesis puts police behavior in the ghetto a decade ago at the active killing of the nonwhite disease stage. His is a frightening exposition. That fear is a backdrop to the analysis in *The Police and the Ghetto*.

NOTES

CHAPTER 1: INTRODUCTION

1. *Report of the National Advisory Commission on Civil Disorders* (New York: Bantam, 1968) p. 266.
2. James Q. Wilson, *Thinking About Crime* (New York: Vintage, 1977), pp. 20 21.
3. Richard Quinney, *Class, State, and Crime* (New York: David McKay Co., 1977), p. 7.
4. Kenneth B. Clark, "The Negro and the Urban Crisis," in *Agenda for America*, Kermit Gordon, ed. (Washington: Brookings Institute, Doubleday, 1969), p. 118.
5. John R. Howard, *The Cutting Edge* (Philadelphia: Lippincott, 1974), p. 42.
6. Wilson, pp. 48-49.
7. Quinney, pp. 9-10.
8. Alexander B. Smith and Harriet Pollack, *Crime and Justice in a Mass Society* (San Francisco: Rinehart Press, 1973), p. 50.
9. Arthur Niederhoffer and Alexander B. Smith, *New Directions in Police-Community Relations* (Hinsdale, Illinois: Dryden Press, 1974), p. 35.
10. Arthur Niederhoffer, *Behind the Shield* (New York: Doubleday, 1969), p. 180.
11. Henry A. Singer, "Police Action—Community Action," *Journal of Social Issues*, vol. 21, no. 1, 1975, p. 99.
12. Wilson, pp. 109-10.
13. Stan Cross and Edward Renner, "An Interaction Analysis of Police-Black Relations," in *Police Community Relations*, Alvin Cohn and Emilo Viano, eds. (New York: Lippincott, 1976), p. 226.
14. William Graham Sumner, *Folkways: A Study of the Sociological Importance of Usages, Manners, Customs, Mores, and Morals* (Boston: Ginn, 1940).
15. Stanford M. Lyman, *The Black American in Sociological Thought* (New York: Capricorn Books, G. P. Putnam, 1973), p. 86.
16. Jerome H. Skolnick, "The Police and the Urban Ghetto," in *The Ambivalent Force*, Arthur Niederhoffer and Abraham S. Blumberg, eds. (Hinsdale, Illinois: Dryden Press, 1976), p. 218.
17. Paul Chevigny, *Police Power* (New York: Vintage, 1969).
18. Kenneth B. Clark, *Dark Ghetto* (New York: Harper & Row, 1967), p. 11.

19.   Harry H. L. Kitano, *Race Relations* (Englewood Cliffs, N.J.: Prentice-Hall, 1974), p. 138.
20.   Robert E. Park, *Human Communities* (Glencoe, Illinois: Free Press, 1952), p. 196.
21.   Robert E. Park, "The City: Suggestions for the Investigation of Human Behavior," in *Classic Essays on the Culture of Cities,* Richard Sennett, ed. (New York: Appleton-Century Crofts, 1969), pp. 129-30.
22.   Martin Luther King, Jr., *Where Do We Go From Here* (New York: Bantam, 1967), p. 42.
23.   Paul Jacobs, *Prelude to Riot* (New York: Random House, 1968), p. 3.

CHAPTER 2: SOCIALIZATION

1.   Joseph Fink and Lloyd G. Sealy, *The Community and the Police—Conflict or Cooperation* (New York: Wiley & Sons, 1974), p. 4.
2.   Smith and Pollack, *Crime and Justice,* pp. 4-5.
3.   Fink and Sealy, pp. 4-5.
4.   *New York Post,* November 12, 1968, p. 53.
5.   Niederhoffer, *Behind the Shield,* pp. 43-44.
6.   Ibid., p. 46.
7.   Ibid., p. 11.
8.   Jerome H. Skolnick and J. Richard Woodsworth, "Bureaucracy, Information, and Social Control: A Study of a Morals Detail," in *The Police: Six Sociological Essays,* David Bordua, ed. (New York: Wiley & Sons, 1967), p. 100.
9.   Niederhoffer, *Behind the Shield,* p. 14.
10.   James Q. Wilson, *Varieties of Police Behavior* (New York: Atheneum, 1975), p. 69.
11.   Ibid., p. 75.
12.   Robert M. Igleburger, John E. Angell, and Gary Pence, "Changing Urban Police: Practitioners' View," in *Police Community Relations,* p. 37.
13.   Ibid., p. 37.
14.   Ibid., p. 38.
15.   John A. Webster, "Police Task and Time Study," *Journal of Criminal Law, Criminology, and Police Science,* March 1970.
16.   Rodney Stark, *Police Riots* (Belmont, California: Wadsworth, 1972), pp. 89-90.
17.   Jerome H. Skolnick, *Justice Without Trial* (New York: Wiley & Sons, 1966), p. 44.
18.   "Study Finds Various 'Frustrations' Affecting Efficiency of New York City Policemen," *New York Times,* June 6, 1977, p. 33.
19.   Gordon Allport, *The Nature of Prejudice* (Garden City, New York: Doubleday, 1958), pp. 283-84.
20.   Victor A. Thompson, *Modern Organization* (New York: Knopf, 1961), p. 15.
21.   Stark, p. 97.

CHAPTER 3: INSTITUTIONAL ATTENDANTS

1.   Howard S. Becker, *Outsiders* (New York: Free Press, 1966), pp. 155-63.
2.   Ibid.
3.   Peter Maas, *Serpico* (New York: Viking, 1973).
4.   Max Weber, *The Theory of Social and Economic Organization* (New York: Free Press, 1964), p. 239.
5.   Colin E. De'Ath and Peter Padbury, "Brokers and the Social Ecology of Minority Groups," in *Ethnic Encounters* (North Scituate, Mass.: Duxbury Press, 1977), pp. 187-88.

6. Allan Silver, "The Demand for Order in Civil Society," in *The Police: Six Sociological Essays*, David J. Bordua, ed. (New York: Wiley & Sons, 1967).
7. Franz Fanon, "Violence and Decolonization," in *Race, Ethnicity and Social Change*, John Stone, ed., (North Scituate, Mass.: Duxbury Press, 1977), p. 233.
8. "Squad Cars Turn into Classrooms as Professors Study Life in Bronx," *New York Times*, May 24, 1977, p. 37.
9. Max Weber, "Class, Status, Party," in *From Max Weber*, Hans Gerth and C. Wright Mills, eds. (New York: Oxford University Press, 1967), pp. 180-95.
10. Jerry D. Rose, *Peoples: The Ethnic Dimension in Human Relations* (Chicago: Rand McNally, 1976), p. 103.
11. George Eaton Simpson and J. Milton Yinger, *Racial and Cultural Minorities: An Analysis of Prejudice and Discrimination* (New York: Harper & Row, 1972), p. 185.
12. Solomon Gross, "The Police of the Twenty-Third Precinct and the East Harlem Community," *Journal of Social Issues*, vol. 31, no. 1, 1975, p. 150.

CHAPTER 4: POLICE ROLES—WHITE ACTORS

1. Max Weber, *The Sociology of Religion* (Boston: Beacon Press, 1963).
2. James Baldwin, *Nobody Knows My Name* (New York: Dell, 1962), p. 62.
3. Max Weber, The *Protestant Ethic and the Spirit of Capitalism* (New York: Scribner's, 1958), pp. 79-92.
4. "Critic-Cop Disarms Bankers," *New York Post*, June 15, 1977, p. 33.
5. Samuel F. Yette, *The Choice* (New York: Berkeley Medallion Books, 1972), p. 213.
6. "Chicago's Feared 'Stone' Gang: Where Are They Now?" *News World*, June 20, 1978, p. 7A.
7. "PAL Essayist Wins a Day as Top Cop," *New York Post*, June 9, 1978, p. 2.
8. "Decline in Crime Rate is Reported; May Aid Renewal of Central Cities," *New York Times*, June 25, 1978, p. 1.
9. "Poll: Police Are Not Effective," *New York Post*, May 12, 1977, p. 24.
10. "Murders By Friends and Relatives Found Rising in New York," *New York Times*, June 25, 1978, p. 1.
11. "Fuzzy Crime Statistics," *New York Times*, September 18, 1977, section 4, p. 3.
12. "How City Defuses its Unstable Cops," *New York Post*, May 31, 1978, p. 17.
13. "Ethics Study for Cops is Slashed 50 Percent," *New York Post*, May 22, 1978, p. 13.
14. Emile Durkheim, *Suicide* (New York: Free Press, 1951), pp. 217-40.
15. Ibid., p. 221.

CHAPTER 5: POLICE ROLES—BLACK ACTORS

1. Nathan Glazer, "America's Race Paradox," in *Nation of Nations*, Rosen, ed. (New York: Random House, 1972), pp. 165-80.
2. Chevigny, *Police Power*, pp. 137-38.
3. E. Franklin Frazier, *Black Bourgeoisie* (Glencoe, Illinois: Free Press, 1957).
4. Gerald W. Lunch, "Black-White Relations Among Policemen in the United States," *Police Journal*, January 1974.
5. "Many Black Policemen Feel They're Between Two Guns," *New York Times*, July 18, 1978, p. B1.
6. "Probe Cops Who Took Shots at Black Officers in Mixup," *New York Post*, July 31, 1978, p. 11.
7. "1968," CBS (TV) News Special, anchored by Harry Reasoner, aired August 25, 1978.

8. Robert L. Derbyshire, "The Social Control Role of the Police in Changing Urban Communities," in *Crime in the City*, Daniel Glaser, ed. (New York: Harper & Row, 1970), pp. 210-18.
9. "Black Cop Hits Bias on Force in Book," *New York Post*, July 5, 1978, p. 14.
10. Erving Goffman, *The Presentation of Self in Everyday Life* (Garden City, New York: Doubleday, 1959).
11. *From Max Weber*, pp. 196-244.
12. R.D. Laing, *The Politics of Experience* (New York: Ballantine, 1967), p. 34.

CHAPTER 6: THE VIEW FROM THE GHETTO

1. James Baldwin, *Notes of a Native Son* (Boston: Beacon Press, 1957), pp. 57-58.
2. Philip M. Stern and George de Vincent, *The Shame of a Nation* (New York: Ivan Oblensky, 1965), pp. 87-88.
3. Thomas Pynchon, "A Journey into the Mind of Watts," in *American Society Since 1945*, William L. O'Neill, ed. (Chicago: Quadrangle, 1969), p. 223.
4. *The Me Nobody Knows*, Stephen M. Joseph, ed. (New York: Discus, 1969), p. 62.
5. Ulf Hannerz, *Soul Side* (New York: Columbia University Press, 1969), p. 162.
6. Ibid., p. 163.
7. *United States Commission on Civil Rights, Number V: Justice* (Washington, D.C., 1961), p. 267.
8. George Edwards, *The Police on the Urban Frontier* (New York: Institute of Human Relations Press, 1968), p. 30.

CHAPTER 7: CONCLUSION

1. Allan Silver, "The Demand for Order in Civil Society," in *The Police: Six Sociological Essays*, p. 7.
2. Edward Shils, "The Theory of Mass Society," *Diogenes*, 1962, pp. 53-54.